Web-Based
Network Management:
Beyond the Browser

Web-Based Network Management: Beyond the Browser

Curt Harler

Wiley Computer Publishing

John Wiley & Sons, Inc.

NEW YORK · CHICHESTER · WEINHEIM · BRISBANE · SINGAPORE · TORONTO

Publisher: Robert Ipsen

Editor: Carol A. Long

Managing Editor: Micheline Frederick

Text Design & Composition: North Market Street Graphics

Designations used by companies to distinguish their products are often claimed as trademarks. In all instances where John Wiley & Sons, Inc., is aware of a claim, the product names appear in initial capital or ALL CAPITAL LETTERS. Readers, however, should contact the appropriate companies for more complete information regarding trademarks and registration.

This book is printed on acid-free paper. ∞

This publication is designed to provide accurate and authoritative information in regard to the subject matter covered. It is sold with the understanding that the publisher is not engaged in professional services. If professional advice or other expert assistance is required, the services of a competent professional person should be sought.

Library of Congress Cataloging-in-Publication Data:

Harler, Curt, 1950–
    Web-based network management : beyond the browser / Curt Harler.
      p.   cm.
    "Wiley Computer Publishing."
    Includes bibliographical references and index.
      ISBN 0-471-32739-5 (pa. : alk. paper)
      1. Wide area networks industry.   2. Local area networks industry.
    3. Computer networks—Management.   I. Title.
    HD9696.2.A2H37   1999
    658'.0546—dc21   99-18066
                                                                        CIP

Printed in the United States of America.

10 9 8 7 6 5 4 3 2 1

Contents

Preface

Save yourself time. Save your company money. Make your operation a better place to work. Look into Web-based network management.

Web-Based Network Management: Beyond the Browser is a one-stop read for the nontechnical or professional network manager who is assessing Web-based network management products. Written in plain English, it is aimed at helping network managers and those working at the immediate levels below and above them understand the concept of Web-based network management. The core of this book is a valuable resource locator of commercial vendors who manufacture products aimed at the Web-based network management market.

Although there are helpful sections discussing Java, Remote MONitoring (RMON) and RMON-2, disaster recovery, and network security, the main thrust of this book is to help the working network manager locate commercial resources. *Web-Based Network Management: Beyond the Browser* will make implementation of any Web-based system simpler and faster. It will be especially helpful to organizations that are approaching the Request for Proposal (RFP) or Request for Quotation (RFQ) stage of the purchase process. The text chapters will serve as a handy touchstone to help assure the right bases have been covered. The vendor listing will provide a valuable resource for contacting reliable companies in the business.

If you classify yourself as an intermediate or advanced network manager, it is likely that a quick skim of the early chapters will be enough. If you are just getting up to speed in this area, read them before delving into a more in-depth technical book. The first chapter of this book outlines the case for Web-based network management. Unless you are in love with long work hours, tedious drives into the office in the middle of the night, or interrupted vacations, you'll probably spend most of your time with the first chapter nodding your head in agreement.

However, this book is not a sales pitch for Web-based management. Chapter 2 takes a good look at many of the negatives and challenges that must be dealt with in any Web-based system. Chief among the challenges is the considerable security risk incurred when any Web-based system is implemented. Opening a network to outside access always is a risky business. Chapter 3 presents an overview of how to deal with security concerns and looks into the disaster-recovery aspects of a Web-based management system.

No matter what your level of expertise or desire for background, spend the bulk of your time with the listings in Chapter 4. It is there that you will be able to separate the wheat from the chaff in your search for golden grains of truth about vendor offerings. This book will pay you back for your reading investment many times over with the contact information provided. The listings in Chapter 4 will save you a ton of work in preparing your initial and subsequent searches for Web-based network management tools, as well as establishing a basis for building a contact list for potential vendors.

All of the basic information an Information Systems (IS) department needs about a product can be found in Chapter 4. If Java is important, you'll be able to find all of the Java-enabled products. If Simple Network Management Protocol (SNMP) and RMON are part of your organization's buying criteria, you'll be able to sort out RMON-compliant products. Need to know if a product will work with the current version of your firm's browser? Again, check Chapter 4. It also details other protocols and outlines each product's operating systems compatibility. In short, the typical reader is more apt to wear out the pages in Chapter 4 than to throw them out. Chapter 4 will become a cross between a road map and an encyclopedia for any company making a Web-based management system buying decision. Not only is all of the vital information there, it is well organized and easy to follow.

Even though this book presents all of the key commercial information in a simple format, it is the author's firm belief that vendors have a vested interest—both in the technology and in their own product. What is really important is what real users think about the possibilities and opportunities offered by Web-based management systems. So, we take a look at how real users take advantage of Web-based management. Case studies range from giant utilities and the *New York Times* to a Cleveland-based Internet service provider and a racecar syndicate.

Last, the author and his sources had some fun: Peering into their crystal balls, they came up with some predictions about the direction Web-based network management products and systems will take. You may agree or disagree with some of the observations. But it won't be dull reading.

I offer my thanks to all of the many software engineers, marketing people, and other writers and editors who helped make this task easier by opening their documentation files, contributing white papers, and sharing information with me for use in this book. To them goes any credit for a job well done. Responsibility for editorial errors (and weak jokes) remains mine alone.

A special thanks to my family members for their support during the many sessions when I burned the midnight oil. *Web-Based Network Management: Beyond the Browser* is dedicated with love to my family.

Curt Harler
curt@curtharler.com

1

Web-Based Management: The View from 10,000 Feet

Our trip to the land of Web-based network management won't take too long, but is going to be strange in some spots and fascinating in others. After this chapter, which serves as a sort of "Guide to Web-Based Management in 20 Minutes or Less," we'll take a quick spin around the universe of Web-based management. Included later on the tour will be stops at individual vendor companies to see what kinds of Web-based management products they are developing, a look at commercial enterprises (much like yours) to see the variety of ways they use their Web-based systems in everyday operations, and a look at what next year's trip to the world of Web-based management might bring.

What Web-Based Management Is

Web-based network management is the ability to monitor and actively manage a network, regardless of the location of the network or the network manager, in real time, using the Internet as an access vehicle (Figure 1.1). Of course, as soon as someone sets up an academic-style definition of Web-based management, they'll find a dozen exceptions to the rule. A short,

Figure 1.1   Web-based network management vision.

practical definition might be that Web-based management is any system that allows an administrator to manage the same things ordinarily handled from inside a data center from the comfort of a Web browser. Or, it can be viewed as a system that, when the pager alarm goes off in the middle of the night, does not require the administrator to pull on a pair of pants and trudge off through a sleet storm to a deserted office to fix a problem.

More technically, it is a system that allows the Management Information Systems (MIS) department to leverage Web technology to extend the function of its network management system. It lets a user extend the existing monitoring, configuration, and troubleshooting functions of the corporate network administrators by taking advantage of the natural efficiencies of the browser.

Browsers are that family of handy tools that allow users to move from one World Wide Web (WWW) site to another with ease and efficiency. Browsers read *Hypertext Markup Language* (HTML) and then link the user's computer with the desired site. The WWW site can be anything from a corporate home page to a device on the corporate network.

The primary browsers that one will encounter are Microsoft's Internet

Explorer, Netscape's Navigator, America Online's Internet Explorer—based proprietary browser, and Opera, a new contender which, while offering some advantages, has the major disadvantage of getting to the game well after Microsoft and Netscape have all but divided the field. However, don't worry much about which browser your company has provided. Like anything else, you will get used to using that browser. Almost all of the products listed in Chapter 4 are compatible with Explorer and Navigator. It is best to check which of the several versions are recommended for use with an individual product, however.

There are at least three good reasons for any network manager to look into Web-based systems:

1. *Ease of access.* Web-based systems provide the ability to get to key management sites or components from anywhere in the world where one can hook up a laptop. It is difficult to imagine an office, even in the more remote parts of the world, that does not have the ability to connect to the Web. Most homes in industrialized societies have computers with some sort of Internet access—in fact, most executives will admit that their home computer is far more advanced than the one they have at the office. Those in technology positions usually have state-of-the-art equipment. The point is not to feel sorry for the technologically impaired in the office as much as it is to point out that the Web-based network manager is likely to be able to get the job done even from a relative's family room. Even better, it is quite possible to carry a network management access node along under one's arm. The laptop computer industry has assured everyone of the ability to take machines along with them.

2. *Platform freedom.* There is no need to scatter Sun workstations or X-terminals in locations that someone considers to be strategic sites today, only to find that tomorrow they are not as convenient or ubiquitous as was once thought. As previously mentioned, the goal is to bring network access to the worker, not to force the worker to move or travel to a network access node. In addition to easing the physical requirement of moving to a preapproved location for access, Web-based management systems generally provide access once a user finds a computer link—any link. Even in a strange location, on an unfamiliar computer, in an emergency the network manager can put together a makeshift management center for the entire corporate network simply by gaining Internet access.

3. *Ease of use.* Simply by adding a bookmark to a computer browser, a network manager can hop to the management component of the sys-

tem under consideration. Almost every Internet tool contains a spot to list *bookmarks* or *favorite places*. These are addresses that a user frequently accesses. Rather than having to enter the entire string of words and numerals that represents the World Wide Web (WWW) address, the user simply gives the site a name (and it can be almost any name the user wants). Later, to return to the site, the user simply clicks on the name of the site and is instantly connected there. On top of the ease of operation, it makes it easy for others (such as assistants) to find the required site. A network manager can talk almost anyone through a check, even if the manager does not have immediate access to a computer or a Web site. The conversation might go like this: "Open up my Explorer. Go to Favorite Places. Scroll down through all of the network areas (forget about the Meg Ryan homepage). Okay, see the line where it says Lancaster Router Network? Click on that. . . ." In a moment the assistant can read off the performance statistics and the problem has at least been defined, if not immediately solved.

At a minimum, you can count on Web-based management to accomplish two things. The obvious one is that it allows for remote management capabilities. However, given the history of network management, this is no small potatoes. No longer is the network manager confined to a specific office or a specialized console. The dream of "anywhere, anytime" management has been realized. The work comes to the worker, rather than the worker having to move to the work.

The second thing—and perhaps more important to companies growing through the acquisition of other firms with dissimilar operating systems—is that it provides platform independence for the management console to a degree that has never before been possible.

No longer does the manager have to learn a new access mechanism for every type of equipment and every brand of equipment in the house. This allows the network manager to put together a best-of-breed solution without having to worry about training another individual on how to access each and every manageable box or system in the network.

Web-Based System Flavors

For purposes of convenience, we can divide Web-based network management systems into three broad areas. The first is a system that allows the management of a number of different devices, made by a variety of manu-

Internet
Protocol (IP)
Master key

Proprietary
One key for one door

Figure 1.2 Web-based network management functionality.

facturers, all under the same general umbrella. Obviously, these are among the most powerful products for Web-based management activity. They allow the manager a sweeping view of the network and give the most functionality (Figure 1.2).

The second group of Web-based network management systems is product-line specific. This is, by far, the category into which the largest number of products fit. There is a reason for this: The vendor has control over the software and hardware development of an internal product. The management system only has to deal with the known components of the system developed by the manufacturer. Whether the product is Simple Network Management Protocol–(SNMP) compatible or not is irrelevant. The manufacturer only has to design a Web-based interface that will work with the product at hand. This does not diminish the capacity of the product—especially if the box resides in a key area of the network, requires frequent monitoring or adjustment, or is prone to need to be reset at odd hours of the day.

Today's Management Requirements

The growth of corporate intranets and the near-universal use of Transmission Control Protocol/Internet Protocol (TCP/IP) for all kinds of local and global needs has given rise to additional management requirements for Domain Name Service (DNS) servers, Dynamic Host Configuration Protocol (DHCP) servers, and Lightweight Directory Access Protocol (LDAP) servers.

Psychologists will tell you that the reason humans feel driven to name dogs, geographic landmarks, ships, and even body parts is that naming imparts ownership and control. If you have a name for something, you have control over it.

The same holds true for networks. On most networks, the truly major management hassles arise, not when there is a node down, but when some unnamed or unidentified device or network segment begins to affect the performance of the network as a whole. More often than network managers would like to admit, there are unknown, undocumented physical segments on their networks. Once all of the devices and nodes have been identified, the use of management protocols becomes a practical solution to handling the network.

To take one example, DHCP allows for automatic TCP/IP configuration. It provides both dynamic and static address allocation across a network and for management of that network. Forget about the technical part of the explanation—the key point to notice is TCP/IP's last name: *IP*. IP is *Internet Protocol*. IP is the software that tracks the Internet addresses of nodes, routes the outgoing message, and recognizes incoming messages. This, then, is the key to connecting networks at Level 3 and higher. It enables the gateways to function.

The gateway, of course, is any inbound or outbound access point on a network. In our case, the gateway is the front door or main access point from the network manager's computer to the Web. Unlike the front door to one's house, which stays in one place, the Web-based network manager's front door travels wherever one can take a laptop computer and find a phone jack to plug into and get a dial tone. At the other end, the network remains in place—however, the Web is smart enough to be able to draw a direct line between the wandering manager and the specified network.

The third group of Web-based network management systems does not deserve the cachet of the first two groups, but these systems are so commonplace that they must be mentioned. These are the products that allow Remote MONitoring (RMON) over the Internet, but fall short in the area of allowing full, active management and reconfiguration. That is, the network manager can access the system over the Web and see what the problem is or review the status of the network. However, these products do not allow Web-based resolution of problems unless they have been Web-enabled by the manufacturer or by some further tweaking at the user's end. Do not make the mistake of dismissing this last category out of hand. RMON and RMON2 will be discussed later in this book. RMON-based products have value in networks. It is highly likely that, since RMON is Simple Network Management Protocol (SNMP)-based, we will see more non-Web RMON products becoming Web-enabled as Web-based management becomes more ubiquitous.

Advantages of Web-Based Systems

There are so many more advantages than disadvantages to Web-based management that it is surprising that everyone has not hopped on the bandwagon already. Web-based management is a bit like skiing. Sure, you could break a leg if you're careless, but with proper training, a few lessons, guidance from an expert, the right equipment, and some get-up-and-go, skiing opens up a whole world of winter beauty and exercise (not to mention spas, saunas, and spiced wine in front of huge stone fireplaces). The same holds true for establishing a Web-based management system. There are a couple of pitfalls that can catch the unaware or uninformed. But the benefits are so many, and so compelling, that it is no wonder that the companies mentioned in Chapter 4 are uniformly bullish about the future of their Web-based products. Even many companies with proprietary solutions recognize the value of allowing network management over the Internet. First, however, let's take a look at how the Web is structured.

The basic unit of information accessible over the Web is a *page.* A program that enables a user to connect to a computer, retrieve a page from it, and display it is known as a *Web browser.* In most applications, the Web uses the standard *client/server model,* where the browser runs on a client (or user) computer that connects to a central server. Think of the client as a customer in a restaurant and the server as the waiter. The client asks for something and the server goes out to where it is stored. In computer terms, the server and the storage facility often are one and the same. A Web server program runs on the server computer. It retrieves the requested data and forwards it to the client. The browser displays that data on the client's computer.

The most common format for displaying Web pages is Hypertext Markup Language (HTML). The HTML format identifies information on a page and tells the browser how to display the page. For example, HTML is what makes some of the words on the page larger than others, presents some in color, and presents others as a flashing or streaming block of type. HTML also will account for a variety of multimedia formats such as pictures, audio, animation, and the like, in addition to blocks of type.

Hypertext Transfer Protocol (HTTP) is the protocol used for communication between the browser and the Web server. Since the server usually runs as a daemon process, the Web server sometimes is called the *HTTP daemon* or just HTTPD.

Web pages can be linked to each other using *hyperlinks,* which are basically computer-friendly road maps that point from one page to another. The endpoints on hyperlinks are called *Uniform Resource Locators* (URLs). A URL uniquely identifies a page somewhere on the WWW. A URL consists of three parts: (1) the protocol that must be used to retrieve the page (almost always HTTP); (2) the name of the computer, server, or other piece of equipment where the page is stored; and (3) the location of the specified page on that other device. Users go from one page to another by following a hyperlink. One of the real values of Web-based management is that any piece of Web-centric equipment can be assigned a URL, and this makes it easy to interact with equipment over the WWW. Users can access a page directly, if they know its URL, by telling the browser to go to the desired URL.

Another way to reach a page is via *Web search.* A number of commercial search engines are available to do the job. They let users search for information on the Web in a variety of ways. A *search engine* is simply a program that takes a user's request as input and generates a Web page that satisfies the request. Programs such as these are interfaced to the Web server running on a machine using an interface called *Common Gateway Interface* (CGI). CGI permits the programs of many formats such as native binaries, shell scripts, perl scripts, and so on. CGI merely establishes a convention for passing input and output between the Web server and the program.

Cost Savings

There are real advantages to being able to see a problem before actually heading off to the user's site to fix it. Clicking on a browser and being transported across the Internet to the device's management screen allows a technician or manager to see the current situation of the device before going out to make repairs. A lot of field time and technician time can be saved if the person knows ahead of time where to look for a specific problem (diagnosis usually requires more than half the time it takes to fix a problem and is often more than half the mental battle). In addition, the proper analysis tools, cards, or cabling equipment can be toted out to the site so the repair is made on the first visit and does not require callbacks.

In many cases, the network management software will allow a remote fix. Take for example a modem which needs to be reset. It is Saturday night, and someone at the office in Poughkeepsie has been burning the midnight oil, but now they can't modem in all the valuable work they have done. A technician or manager with Internet access can check and confirm the problem. In many cases, the technician can make a change simply by clicking a few icons on the network management screen. Voilá—problem solved in Poughkeepsie as well as for the technician.

The technician can be on call, rather than on site. A 15-minute task does not require 8 hours of weekend pay.

In almost every one of these cases, the argument for Web-based management can be reduced to terms of dollar savings. Even in those instances where the benefit accrues to the individual technicians who do not have to drag themselves away from home on a rainy night, a sizable dollar savings is eventually realized as the workers' job satisfaction remains high and there is less expense incurred in rehiring and retraining workers, unexcused absenteeism, and similar human resources costs.

Why MIS Must Consider Web-Based Management

Let's face it: The bottom line on any information systems management decision comes down to the bottom line. If a decision can not be justified to the CIO or the CFO based on return to the organization, generally in excess of what could be expected from investing the money elsewhere, it simply is not going to happen.

Depending on the operations being outfitted with a Web-based network management system, it may be possible to justify the additional expense of a Web-based tool simply on the speedier time for restoration. The term *mission critical* is probably the most overused term in the industry. It is stamped on everything (bringing back to mind a shipment of ruggedized steel tool cases that were shipped into a firm, each carefully marked "fragile/handle with care"). However, there are a number of mission-critical applications in every operation. In reservations centers, some banking operations such as currency exchange, stock and commodities markets, and other applications, the loss of a few minutes up-time on a network will cost the company thousands of dollars. Speed of restoration is everything. While most IS nerve centers are staffed on a 7-by-24 (7 × 24) basis, being able to provide Web-based network management to a key person to analyze a situation may save hours of lost time or productivity as noted in Figure 1.3.

Putting together a budget to justify the few thousands of dollars required to provide fully interactive Web-based capability should be child's play.

Staff time and overtime (if the technicians in your department are on an

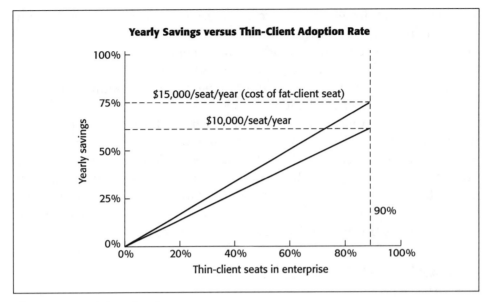

Figure 1.3 Web-based savings.
Source: Sun Microsystems

hourly basis) is another area to include when doing a cost-justification for a Web-based network management system.

Happy Employees

Staff retention is another plus. While nobody will join your team simply because you have implemented a Web-based network management system, it may be one of the small "satisfiers" that allows your department to hire or retain key personnel. If nothing else, it will assure new hires that the department is on the cutting edge of technology and has taken the time to look into and invest in state-of-the-art management systems.

Corporate higher-ups will like the fact that key workers are available to perform their job functions no matter where they are. While no system's health should be dependent on one employee's skills base, Murphy's law says that problems always will happen at the worst possible time, from a staffing point of view. Giving key workers Web-based access for making changes in the network is better than giving them pagers or cell phones. Having Web-based access to the network means that technicians and managers (whether in a remote office, at a hotel across the country, or vacationing in Cancun) can actually do something about a problem.

Decisions and Flexibility

Now we get to the good part: reducing your daily stress as a result of not being able to meet all of the previously mentioned goals.

As a reader of this book, you are probably computer literate. In fact, it is likely that you are way off the right end of the bell curve when it comes to computer literacy—which means that almost everyone else in your organization is probably far behind your ability to handle C++ and other esoteric languages. Unless you want to be tied to your desk or to an electronic leash such as a pager, it would be well to implement a network management system that allows at least Level 1 decisions to be made quickly and easily.

When the automobile first became a commercial product, any driver had to be a mechanic and an engineer, as well. A breakdown required the ability to fix the vehicle on the spot. Major problems meant some on-site jury rigging to engineer a solution to the problem. Those days are long gone. Today, one expects to hop into the car, turn a key, and drive.

The same is true of a network. Users at all levels want to be able to use the system without having to hassle with a host of access problems.

Full-function Web access adds significant flexibility in viewing service-level status information. Also key is the availability of remote access for highly skilled, off-shift personnel. The process includes a relational database engine that sifts through vast amounts of statistical data, homogenizes it into a common presentation format, and generates automated reports that correlate events in an enterprisewide view of the network.

Internet-Based Network Monitoring Is Growing

The META Group estimates that the network performance analysis and reporting market will grow from $120 million in 1997 to $700 million in the year 2000. The Reston, Virginia-based industry analysis firm is bullish on the future of the performance analysis industry, based largely on the number of Fortune 1000 companies, Internet service providers (ISPs), and telecommunications firms that are moving toward broad-based installation of network monitoring equipment.

Many information systems departments require that a long, drawn-out process be followed when an individual user or work group wants additional bandwidth. With a Web browser, the network manager can change bandwidth allocations to meet the needs of a department (finance, accounting, or engineering) or Internet traffic (File Transfer Protocol [FTP], e-mail, and Web access). Keep in mind that users are concerned not only about the quantity of bandwidth available but also the quality.

Providing quality control and measurable results allows you to bill back to individual departments based on quality of service (QoS).

Guaranteeing QoS is one way to improve the lot of those using any network, especially critical or real-time Internet-based applications. The way for a service provider or IT manager to back up those guarantees is by using a SONET network, which assures quick time to restoration and an acceptable level of network performance.

The next wave will be multiservice platforms which demand high bandwidth and will have to give multifunctional services at full speed. If it does not perform at wire speed, it's broken. Control over the network should be provided at the access point since the day is not far off when Internet-based bandwidth at 155 Mb/s will be commonplace to customers, who then will control the breakdown of the data stream.

Depending on the day of the week, the approach of a shouting coworker with an unknown problem to solve can be viewed as either another exciting challenge to make the hours go by faster or the start of a three-Excedrin afternoon.

Internet-based network monitoring allows you to reach out into all areas of the network and anticipate and solve network problems before they become disasters. Would it not be a lot more fun to greet your coworker with a cheery, "Hey, Jim, why didn't you tell me you were having some problems on the Omaha node? Is it working better since we fixed it a few minutes ago? What is it you need now?" and watch him slink back to his cubicle, having lost the opportunity to blame his low productivity on the IS department?

Characteristics of Good Systems

A good Web-based system will be able to provide automated information gathering in at least three key areas: (1) device discovery and configuration (or reconfiguration), (2) data analysis, and (3) report generation.

Device Discovery and Configuration

There is no feeling more hopeless than being faced with a network that never was well documented and being forced to find a place to start to manage the network. The feeling is like being lost in a strange city at night where one does not speak the language. Any direction one starts to take will almost certainly lead to the wrong place. However, many software products will go out and actively document the devices on the network and check their configurations. While not 100 percent foolproof, it's a great place to start—almost like having a guidebook in hand.

Data Analysis

The data analysis portion of the product is usually the one that a user is most apt to expect from a network management tool. That is the key function of a Web-based management system. However, it is the third aspect that is usually taken for granted and that often ends up being the major dissatisfaction a network manager has with a product: report generation.

Report Generation

Reports may be likened to a tour guide. A good guide talks your language, understands the sights you want to see, and relates to special interests such as art museums or historical sites. Surely every Web-based management product displays or prints out reports (Figure 1.4). You need to ask yourself the following questions:

- Are they in a language or presentation format that you understand?
- Do those reporting devices take you to the parts of the network you want to view?

TYPE	FORMAT	USAGE
Tabular	Information is displayed as alpha numeric and numeric text in columns and rows.	Select this format when you're using the information as a stand-alone report.
Graphical	Information is displayed in graph format with a corresponding legend.	Select this format when you're using the information as a stand-alone report.
Comma-separated value (CSV)	Information is displayed as alpha numeric and numeric text in strings, with values separated by commas.	Select this format when you plan to import the information into a spreadsheet-type application.
Tab-separated value (TSV)	Information is displayed as alpha numeric and numeric text in strings, with values separated by a tab character.	Select this format when you plan to import the information into a spreadsheet-type application.

Figure 1.4 Report formats.

Source: NetScout Systems

- Are they flexible enough to take you to one area today and to a different one tomorrow?

- Are they intelligent enough to sort out special interests on the network (say, only routers) and not force you to put up with a pile of extraneous reports to get to the places on the network you want to see?

It is not only the end user who benefits from a well-designed Web-based management package. There are benefits that accrue to the manufacturers of Web-based systems, too. In this latter case, the main benefit to the vendor is *simplicity.* For example, Cabletron used to produce various products in five flavors of Unix plus Windows NT for every application. There is no doubt that all purchasers had to pay for the additional development time, regardless of which system they were interested in purchasing.

Web Friendliness

Writing for the Web simplifies things. While hard-core systems administrators like Unix, the Web is an interface that everyone with a degree of computer literacy knows and loves. Even with service-level applications, where the information systems department is dealing with less computer-literate people, one is apt to find some familiarity with Web-based programs. Web-based tools are well suited to people more comfortable clicking a bookmark or favorite places icon than dealing with Unix or Motif.

In addition, vendors can ship product in less time with a lower cost. While the core of the application may still be Unix, the Web wrapper makes life easier for the user.

Vendors are doing their best to promote Web-based network management and to assure some commonality of direction.

Surf Over to WBEM

The Web-Based Enterprise Management (WBEM) multivendor alliance is a broad industry initiative launched in July 1996 by BMC Software Inc., Cisco Systems Inc., Compaq Computer Corp., Intel Corp., and Microsoft Corp. WBEM's goal is to establish Internet Engineering Task Force–(IETF-) approved standards for Web-based network management software. WBEM can be thought of as the Switzerland of the Web-based management buisness. It is the neutral ground where all can meet to resolve technical differences and get a neutral view of where the industry should be headed in the matter of standardization. It has successfully provided standards-based technologies to enable the development of tools and products that reduce the complexity and costs of managing an enterprise computing environment.

The original five companies approved a transfer of the WBEM initiative to the Desktop Management Task Force (DMTF) in early June 1998, complementing the original goals of WBEM to create standards-based technologies that provide the means to create point-solution and end-to-end enterprise management products. Today, the members of WBEM represent the principal group providing leadership to the Web-based network management initiative, although several other emerging alliances are doing a good job of providing standards to allow vendors to develop integrated, platform-independent network management applications.

WBEM details enterprise management standards and related technologies that work with existing management standards like Desktop Management Interface (DMI) and SNMP. WBEM's activities complement other standards by providing a uniform model that represents the managed environment through which management data from any source can be accessed in a common way. This removes the burden on the application writer of creating applications that consume management information from many different sources, all having dissimilar Application Program Interfaces (APIs) and data object models. Instead, applications are written to access management information from a single object model and access point. This makes management applications independent of the specific APIs or standards used to instrument each managed entity, allowing correlation of data and events from multiple sources on a local or enterprisewide basis.

The Common Information Model (CIM) was originally conceived by Microsoft and then adopted and evolved by the DMTF. Today, it is a published WBEM standard which is developed in open forum by DMTF member companies.

The CIM object-oriented schema standardized by the DMTF offers a single data description mechanism for all enterprise data sources. The power of this model is a key part of the WBEM initiative. By offering a standard schema that supports inheritance, vendors (data publishers) can offer standard data classes and properties, while also allowing vendor-specific extensions to be derived differentiating specific products. The schema also allows associations to be built between objects described by the model, regardless of the original data source. DMI data regarding a local area network (LAN) card can therefore be associated with the SNMP data from the relevant LAN port, and the system-level protocol bindings can be reported by the platform APIs. This combination allows management solutions at the administrative level to follow the trail of a fault or performance problem from its reported location (a user's application error) to the actual problem (a faulty repeater card) by walking the associations within the schema and the WBEM aggregation points in the network.

This has the added benefit of allowing enterprise management solutions to be created without vendor-specific or multiprotocol dependencies at the management application level.

WBEM Standards

WBEM products interoperate in a multisystem environment by using technologies designed around WBEM standards. When Microsoft developed its common, object-based information model called *HMMS,* it was adopted by the DMTF and evolved into the Common Information Model (CIM), now published as the *CIMv2* schema. The DMTF plans to develop and publish additional WBEM standards so that WBEM products that manage heterogeneous systems, regardless of their instrumentation mechanisms, can be developed by management vendors. The WBEM name is a familiar industry term, and the DMTF will use that moniker when publishing future DMTF WBEM standards that provide for interoperable management of the enterprise.

The HMMP interchange mechanism proposed by Microsoft early in the WBEM initiative was a placeholder for a standards-based, environment-independent means of communicating CIM information between heterogeneous systems. Industry developments in the standardization of XML, a technique for representing structured data in a platform-neutral way, have presented the WBEM initiative with new opportunities to standardize WBEM's cross-platform remoting of CIM objects. Microsoft is on record as supporting this direction.

Because the purpose of this book is to provide an overview, and not a list of technical specifications, those who are interested in the standards can investigate to the WBEM discussion list. It is the best place to get tuned into what is happening. The discussion list is a majordomo-operated, unmoderated e-mail exploder that provides a forum for general discussion on all aspects of WBEM. The name of the list is wbem-discussion@freerange.com.

All of the original WBEM companies, DMTF member companies, and many others who have an interest in WBEM standards and technologies are members of the list. If you have a question on WBEM, they invite you to send a message to the list. The list operates much like a newsgroup, with no particular company or person responsible for answering questions posted to the list. However many WBEM-related issues have been discussed and resolved on the list. This list is a good source of information on WBEM's progress as new WBEM standards and technologies are announced.

To subscribe or remove yourself from the WBEM discussion list, please e-mail benjamin@freerange.com.

Network Lifestyle Fit

The most common software on desktop computers today is not Lotus 1-2-3. It is not some obsolete version of Word. It isn't even Tetras or SIM City. It's a browser. Every computer shipped in the past several years has been equipped with a browser that allows users to travel through cyberspace to places far away.

Oh, to be somewhere where we are not. Ever since childhood, most people have had days when they wanted (or needed) to be somewhere else. As children, the state said we had to sit in a classroom when we would have much preferred to be on a ballfield. As adults, we longed to be on the ski slopes while other responsibilities kept us cooped up in an office.

Today, Sunday afternoons are ruined by calls from desperate office workers, all demanding yet another piece of our time to come into the network center and deal with some crisis or another. Network administrators need to be able to manage anything from anywhere.

Until recently, there was no alternative but to apologize to the house guests, promise the kids that you really would take them to the circus next year, and pack off to solve the problem.

Once the poor, harried manager began to look into the problem, it immediately became clear that the network person was convinced that the problem rested with the application. Of course, the applications person swore that the network was at fault. Everyone was focused on their little corners of the universe and nobody had the 10,000-foot view. In fact, it was a rare case when any of the parties involved even bothered to snoop around the other person's domain. Their job, as they seemed to see it, was to prove their innocence and point fingers at the other department.

Fortunately, Web-based network management provides a convenient window for all three parties involved. It is as simple as clicking a browser for the network person to take a look at the application's performance. Likewise, a simple trip across the Web lets the applications administrator evaluate the status of the network. As their supervisor, it is straightforward to look at performance statistics on both sides of the equation.

Pairing reports with specific business practices lets organizations proactively monitor and plan for the network infrastructure necessary to support those business practices, further leveraging the network infrastructure for a competitive advantage.

On top of that, it is necessary to bring the IT staffers to a level where they are able to manage the network to its desired state, or best-case operating level, rather than have them focused on crisis management and fixing crashes. This requires a series of management tools which can adapt to each of the new pieces of hardware, software, applications, and other technology that are added to the computing environment. The network is far-flung, diverse, and dynamic. It requires a medium that is just as widespread geographically, user-friendly despite the technology being used, and able to adjust to the dynamics of the changing network scene.

Microsoft Match

The network operating system of choice for many companies is Microsoft's *Windows NT Server*. While it is a robust offering, it also has brought a whole new encumbrance on the IS/IT team, requiring management and administration of networks in far-flung locations. Even administration of a LAN (nominally, a *local area* network) may require remote capability. Campus-area and wide area networks certainly require remote management of the network. The complexity of these networks has made user administration a significant task.

Quality of Service Demands

Proper management of a network requires control and direction to ensure that it delivers authorized services at the correct time to individuals who are approved for a host of levels of Quality of Service (QoS). A major part of QoS is being able to provide the service in a prompt and thorough manner and being able to dynamically adjust the service provided to a customer to assure that QoS is maintained (Figure 1.5). This can include anything from domain management, rebooting a remote terminal, or providing additional bandwidth to assuring that the latest versions of client software are distributed throughout the organization without requiring a worker to visit each site or each computer.

The Internet Factor

The CEO of a well-known networking startup maintains that the Internet is evolving into the new public network, and those that take advantage of

QoS REQUIREMENT	
QoS REQUIREMENT	**CBQ**
Traffic classification	Enterprise customers can classify traffic flows based on internal business priorities.
Traffic shaping	The network edge device explicitly rate-shapes traffic to meet customer- or business-defined policies.
Policing	Traffic is subject to trusted control at the network edge to limit traffic flows that would violate the agreed service contracts.
Prioritization	It is possible to prioritize use of bandwidth to ensure bandwidth is available for the most important time-sensitive or business-critical traffic flows.
Measurement	Enterprises and network providers can accurately measure bandwidth usage to ensure it is effectively allocated and delivered.
Provisioning	The customer controls bandwidth allocations to support the dynamic provisioning or access bandwidth according to changing business policies.
Service-level marking	Local traffic flows are mapped to the service levels offered by the network provider to ensure consistent and predictable service.

Figure 1.5 Customer-based quality (CBQ) as an access Quality of Service (QoS) solution.
Source: Xedia Corporation

this trend can achieve a fundamental business advantage. For the Internet to progress from its strengths in connectivity and become a fundamentally reliable infrastructure, advances will have to come both from business drivers and from technology built to solve the critical problems involved in growing networks at unprecedented rates.

Though the Internet is recent, the phenomenon of service adoption of communication services is not. As users reach critical mass, the service must transition from accommodating technologically savvy early adopters to mainstream use.

Market evolution is guiding the Internet to accomplish this goal by segmenting the network into a hierarchy of functions. Core backbone services are becoming distinct from the access-layer and subscriber services. Backbone providers achieve economies of scale by exploiting fundamental scaling advantages in operational cost and network reach, leading to more reliable and economic Internet backbone services.

For the enterprise IT manager, the Internet has much of the flavor of the impact of the PC on business. By giving control and flexibility to the user, rapid evolution in business practice is attained. However, network managers must take responsibility for a level of service that is outside their control. Those network managers who adopt, understand, and optimize these network services will deliver maximum value to their enterprise users.

Efficiency and Detection

Web-based management schemes will be appropriate in any operation where the organization is attempting to create a more efficient administrative model. This can range from client/server-based systems to mainframe computing.

Vendor customers have identified that dependable access to OS/390-based business applications is the major challenge to deploying TCP/IP backbone networks. They want network management products to provide the necessary proactive monitoring, diagnostic, and performance capabilities that enable them to better manage their networks and thereby increase service availability. As engineers often point out, complex systems often fail slowly. Protocols and applications are designed to hide small failures (e.g., packet loss) from the user. If network managers can collect enough data and analyze it for subtle trends, they can see many potential failures while they are in the earliest stages and while they are still hidden from the users. Management information base (MIB) instrumentation provides access to the needed data on the network.

The early stages of network failure often manifest themselves as performance problems—things that should not be permitted to grow. One way to find those problems fast is to be able to access performance data over the Web or to have that data forwarded to a network manager over the Internet.

The Human Element

In considering all of this technology, it would be a major mistake to overlook the human element of network management. There are two major human-element reasons to go with a Web-based management system: preventing downtime and accommodating telecommuting.

Preventing Worker Downtime

The first human-element factor is availability during times when it is difficult for a human to be at the workplace. This might involve, for example, a key engineer who is pregnant or has just delivered a baby and is understandably unwilling to leave home for long periods of time. In such a situation, the engineer can take advantage of Web-based network management as long as she has access to any PC. Or, a network manager might not be able to carve snowboard turns quite as elegantly this year as five years before. The resulting six weeks of immobility or confinement does not have to keep him or her from contributing to the MIS team.

Telecommuting Trend

The second human-element factor of Web-based management growth is the telecommuting trend and its lure for key employees with strong skill sets who greatly benefit the bottom line but either need or want to be off site. As we leave the twentieth-century attitude of people going to work and fall into the twenty-first-century reality of work going to people, management is going to discover that the best and brightest workers will choose where they are going to live, in geographic locations that suit their lifestyles. The Chicago-based company with a good IP-based management system will not lose the services of top-level workers just because they like the Texas lifestyle better. A company located in Fargo, North Dakota, or Laramie, Wyoming, will not have to settle for local talent in its search for network help. The worker who prefers to be near the beaches of California or the theatres of New York City will be fair game for a job because the Web-based system will provide a reach into the company network, wherever it is, from wherever the worker happens to be.

Real-life companies—enterprises with a fair amount of experience in using Web-based management—are in love with the concept, too. We'll look at several of them when our tour of the world of Web-based management gets to Chapter 5. First, however, we'll take a trip to those places where Web-based management does and does not work.

2

Objections to Web-Based Network Management

Chapter 1 should come with a disclaimer. Before anyone gets too hyped up about all of the wonderful things Web-based systems can accomplish, it is only fair to present a warning that there are some concerns, problems, and potential pitfalls in the world of Web-based network management. Just as a tour director would be remiss if he or she failed to warn clients away from marginal restaurants or currency-exchange scams, this book would be remiss if it did not point out some of the practical problems that an IT team can expect to encounter if it makes the move into Web-based management of its network.

If Web-based network management were the endgame of all management concerns, there would be no reason to read the rest of the pages in this book. The MIS manager would simply book passage to the nearest trade show, sign a contract for the product of choice, unravel the shrink wrap on the package, and toss away any concerns about maintaining the organization's network. Just as any vacation has delays, expenses, and even calamities that may have to be overcome, there are challenges to be met as we get our passports stamped on the world tour of Web-based network management, too.

Although a lot of people are bullish enough on the concept of Web-based network management to make this argument, there are a few objections that will be raised internally, by people who have some appreciation for the concerns and challenges faced by running a network. These same questions are ones that you should raise with your local, friendly sales representatives, at least to make them feel that they have done a good job of selling the product.

There are situations in which the network manager on call should not be encouraged to go beyond the doors of the administration center. Configuring the network to allow remote administration only encourages the technicians to go to trade shows, take days off, and otherwise find excuses to manage the network from someplace other than the central site. In short, define the need for remote management and the parameters under which those with access to Web-based management systems will be expected to work. If there is always a well-trained someone in the center on a 24-hour basis, then perhaps the hassle and expense of remote management is not required. But there still will be advantages to be garnered from basing the organization's management platform on the IP protocol.

Few centers have budgets that allow them to be fully staffed, with experts in every system being run, on a 7×24 basis. Even if they do have round-the-clock expertise generally available, it is a fact of life that workers do get sick. They do take time off. They do sleep in after a long, tough weekend. It is easy to see that, even in those cases where qualified management is generally present, a Web-based system may still be required to fill in the staffing gaps that are likely to occur in cases of emergency.

In addition to worrying about the health of the employees, there also are major concerns about the health of the network. In fact, one of the largest single concerns that any administrator should have when considering a remote network polling system of any sort is the amount of network polling traffic that will be generated as the result of the automatic analysis function. This is one case where it is wise to be sure that the cure is not worse than the ailment.

Paralysis by analysis usually refers to the condition encountered by weak decision makers who can not make up their minds until they have analyzed every tiny sort of information available that might throw any light at all on the subject they are analyzing. However, the same paralysis by analysis can be encountered when a company installs a network management system to do performance analysis and monitoring. Especially in networks that are running at or near optimum capacity (and that would appear to be 99 percent of the networks out there), the chances that polling traffic will collide with important message traffic is higher than one might expect. Any network running in the vicinity of 70 percent of load should be suspect, as any surge in traffic could create an excessive demand on the network's capabilities and might bring the network down.

This is not an insurmountable problem by any stretch of the imagination. For one thing, the timing of network management transactions can be set to coincide with the lower-usage hours. Simply avoid doing low-priority jobs during the busy times from 8:00 to 10:00 A.M. and again around 1:30 to 3:30 P.M. Avoiding the hours when most workers are signing onto the network in the morning, and rushing to check e-mail and get work underway after lunch, will reduce the likelihood of extraneous collisions. Network updates, searches for new or pirate equipment on the network, and similar functions should be conducted in the less busy periods. While this may seem like common sense, network operators are prey to the same desires to get work done in the main working hours of the day. Unfortunately, doing low-priority tasks during the crunch hours is one good way to assure that there is a lot more work to be done before it is time to go home. There should be enough to do on the average network without creating collisions and congestion that will only add to the daily burden of network administration.

All of these cautions are valid whether the network management operation in an organization is Web-based or it operates on some other system. Do not simply dismiss the problem of minimizing test-incurred traffic during the busy hours as "common sense." Common sense, unfortunately, is not all that common.

Connectivity Issues

Although today's Internet excels on the dimension of connectivity, it can fall short in the delivery of business-critical reliability and multiple services for user application demands, according to industry leaders. Reliable remote testing capability is one of those key applications. To the IT manager, these are fundamental challenges as business use of the Internet expands. To the network operator, these are manifestations of the special challenge of growing a network at unprecedented rates. While user expectations are shaped by the reliability of the voice network, which is single purpose, mature, and slow growing, the Internet is the frontier of communications services, growing more than 300 percent a year and connecting multiple traffic types, from voice to data.

It is not news that networks are growing like algae blooms on a hot summer day. Many networks are doubling in size every year. With the boom in mergers and acquisitions, it is not unusual for a network manager to be dealing with a network that is much larger by year's end than it was at the start of the year. In growing a network by leaps and bounds each year, multiple network layers must achieve breakthroughs in scale for reliable end-to-end response times. This is not as easy to achieve as it seems on paper. Rarely are the various equipment, bandwidth, personnel, and financial resources expanded at a rate anywhere near equal to the rate of expansion of the network.

Not only must the growth be fast enough to accommodate all of the institutional demands, but it must take place in a logical manner. It is no good to put a supercapacity network into one location if the other locations are unable to handle the traffic it generates. It is futile to put in a system for a given division—say engineering or the financial department—that the current network management scheme can not handle. Even individual components in the network must be manageable by the given network management system. Take a look at all of the elements in the typical corporate or organizational network that must grow rapidly and in a coordinated fashion: These include data sources, both Web servers and databases; the underlying optical layer; core data gear; the access layer; and, finally, network-aware applications. The revolution in fiberoptic technologies, the multiple competing high-speed access technologies such as any Digital Subscriber Lines (xDSL) and cable modems, and recent advances in the design of server farms highlight the need for advances in the core routing layer to alleviate the bottleneck and enable reliable growth. While a Web-based network management system can help manage such growth, it needs to be scaled to meet the demands of tomorrow's network, not today's budget. Web-based management is a great tool. But it is not a miracle cure. Without the proper underpinnings, a Web-based system can fall flat just as easily as can any other network management scheme.

Performance, control of both the internal network and relationships amongst multiple external ISPs for traffic exchange, and traffic engineering tools to optimize the network are fundamental to removing the core routing layer as the bottleneck to reliable Internet growth.

Hiring people who can design, implement, and manage a Web-based system is not a slam dunk, by any means. Computer-literate people with a good understanding of the Web are in great demand. IP is a hot item on any computer person's resume, and the expectation is that IP competence will bring a higher salary to the worker who understands IP. Solving all of the issues with IP enabling the management system will be exacerbated by shortages in experts in the protocols and principles underlying the operation of the Internet as a global and public network. The good news, however, is that only a couple of key individuals need to be completely Internet literate. Most of the other workers on the team will have at least a basic understanding of how to work with and interact with Web-based media. Once the correct URLs have been entered under Favorite Places for the devices to be managed, the everyday workers should have no problem doing their jobs. There will, however, be a need for some level of additional training. That adds another layer of cost and complexity.

With all of the growth of enterprise networks, and the growing concern over how traffic is going to be handled, there is some legitimate concern about what kind of box will eventually be the one carrying network traffic. Despite some of the complications of implementing and learning Web-based systems, the basic idea and foundation of any solid Web-based management system will not be dependent on which device wins out in terms of carrying voice, data, and video traffic. Web-based systems are totally agnostic when it comes to battles between and among the traditional telephone Private Branch Exchange (PBX,) the new Internet Protocol–Private Branch Exchange (IP-PBX,) traffic forwarding by router, or the growing popularity of NT Server. Nor does the platform matter (Windows, NT, UNIX, Linux, etc.). Vendors promise they'll comply with any device or platform. They note that IT and Telecom people want to run their networks at maximum efficiency for the lowest possible cost. Those two goals have not changed one iota in the 20 years that telemanagement systems have been evolving, and they won't change in the next 20 years. Firms want to provide the means for communications managers to get data so that they can make informed decisions about their networks and the people using them.

Most other systems providers strive to have their equipment be transparent in delivering the data. The more their products can integrate with what products network managers use (PBXs, routers, firewalls, spreadsheets, word processor programs, database programs, browsers, e-mail, etc.) the easier it is for them to collect, manipulate, and distribute the data.

While chargeback is a prime reason to purchase telemanagement products, IT is more interested right now in monitoring usage to enforce compliance of corporate policies. Such policy-based management might be targeted as ensuring that John Doe doesn't stay online for more than two hours a day. Or, it might provide a check to ensure that Jane Doe uses the local phone number to dial in rather than an 800 number. Of course, inventory, work orders, trouble tickets, cable management, and toll-fraud detection and avoidance are other big reasons for using telemanagement products.

Security Remains a Concern

Security concerns are a valid consideration any time any application is going to be run over the Internet—especially one as critical as monitoring and controlling key devices in the corporate network. It is a sufficiently valid concern that an entire section of this book (in Chapter 3) is devoted to the topic. While some people brush aside such worries with glib watchwords like "firewall protection," the topic deserves serious analysis before moving ahead with any Web-based applications. Keep in mind that simply using the IP protocol does not expose the entire network to any Internet-based danger. But if there is any door to the outside world, regardless of which protocol is being used, there is a legitimate need for a good security program. No matter how the network is set up, if there is any way a person can access your network from outside, security must be in place.

The old adage "What's sauce for the goose is sauce for the gander" applies equally to security situations. If the security of the network is paramount, then providing any opening into that network must be for a vital reason. The basic question becomes: Is the convenience of the network manager worth the security concerns and headaches that providing remote access will incur? Here the cost-benefit analysis is more related to the cost of protection versus all the benefits of remote network management. This is not an attempt to unbalance the decision scales by putting a heavy hand down on the side of Web-based management. There will be cases where the convenience of having a Web-based system will be overridden by the possibility, however remote, of a network intrusion.

Network management is an important task that should not be open to invasion by a malicious user. With Web-based network management, unless adequate precautions are taken, anyone with a Web browser may have the opportunity to access the network management system. Even a mechanism that incorporates password authentication may be susceptible to eavesdropping on the network.

It is possible to provide a reasonable level of security protection. Any network that provides external access at any point is suspect, but if the network's overall security is solid, the network should be safe even if remote management is part of the overall scheme. Most financial networks, for example, have extremely good intrusion protection built into the overall network management plan. The design of the network should allow for specific entry points for such functions as network management. These are not the networks where security is of concern.

Rather, it is the mundane, everyday network that is most at risk—the one that the network manager (and perhaps even corporate management) feels is not at risk from intrusion. In these cases the risk is most often from internal tampering. This can be accidental. A worker might stumble on the Web-based network management system and figure it would be fun to poke around a bit and see what the network is about. Or, that worker might realize what the system is about and decide to reconfigure his or her security access up a level or two to get full T1 access to the Internet or see what the sales manager earns each quarter. The intrusion might be malicious: A disgruntled employee with a bit of networking knowledge might decide to get back at the company by going home at night and reconfiguring a few nodes here and shutting down a few links there.

There is irony here. Should the latter scenario be the case, it is likely that the only way the company will be able to restore the troubled network quickly is if the network manager has remote access to it.

Any situation that would require sending sensitive company information out over a dial-up link is open to trouble. Without strong security, such an environment is potentially open to data thieves and vulnerable to loss. The solution is to try to provide dedicated tools and technology that will allow an administrator to function effectively from home or from the road.

The scenarios are endless. The point, however, is to make sure that the network manager is aware of the potential dangers and that the security experts are aware of what is being proposed.

How Fast Can You Go?

Another aspect of the situation, while not completely vetoing the concept of Web-based management, will rear its ugly head in many cases and needs to be dealt with. This is the issue of *access speed.* Industry experts note that there will be a significant difference in the performance of the network once the operation is taken outside the firewall. Many shops will have those power-users who are fortunate enough to have Integrated Services Digital Network (ISDN) access from home (or even a T1 link). But keep in mind that the ultimate vision for Web-based management is to be able to perform tasks from the road. This means hooking the laptop up in a hotel room (and there are a lot of hotel rooms in this country where even the most golden of gold cards will not earn a manager access to a data jack) or to a phone in an airport lounge. With Plain Old Telephone Service (POTS), things are going to happen a lot slower than they will at the fast data speeds attainable on a corporate network.

Depending on the amount of data being transferred in any remote access situation, the cure can be almost as painful as the problem. Many phone connections are painfully inefficient. This can be overcome by systems that incorporate data transport functions. Among the key areas to look at are such things as an effective data compression algorithm, a data-bursting algorithm (which allows data to be transmitted in efficient "bursts" of speed), and a system that allows the removal of repetitive data packets when the transmission is flowing smoothly.

Another significant challenge is handling asynchronous events from network devices. The Web paradigm is based on an asynchronous request from the browser to the Web server, but the response from the server to the browser is synchronous, Wipro engineers point out. Current standards do not accommodate asynchronous communication initiated by the server.

Integration of management applications from device vendors is another area that may pose some difficulty. Some device vendors will be reluctant to develop management applications on a number of different Network Management System (NMS) frameworks. Convincing them to develop management applications under a new Web-based NM framework will be an uphill task. This group will include those who subscribed to the IBM philosophy of the 1960s that no competitor's product line could ever begin to approach theirs in the marketplace, and so there was no need to consider other systems when building a family of products. This same bunch moved into video conferencing and promoted proprietary products until the market demanded open standards. Perhaps the NMS market will learn from the past. It is possible that Web technology will attain a sufficient level of market acceptance and attractiveness to motivate device vendors to develop management applications.

There is some question as to how deeply some vendors are committed to the idea of Web-based management. "Most of the incumbents have been slow to adopt new technologies out of the desire to protect their existing investments," noted *InternetWeek* in its February 23, 1998, article entitled "Insights & Incites." Looking at the new breed of Internet network management solutions, the paper cautioned that players need to understand that recycled Unix-based client/server management solutions are not going to fly in the evolving world of intranets and extranets. "A thin veneer of browser-based access will not suffice in a market that will soon see vendors bragging that they are more Web-based than the rest," the paper warned. "Leveraging the security solutions created by the Web-based electronic commerce market will be critical, as will the use of push technology."

Looking at the Costs

As an example, one networking vendor, NetOps, likes to divide the benefits of Web-based management into two separate camps: ergonomics and economics. The ergonomics part is made up of the convenience of having an entire network recognized, discovered, analyzed, and supervised from one console that all approved players can get into, and that those who are not approved cannot access.

The company notes that there are both hard- and soft-dollar costs and benefits to a well-designed system. NetOps specializes in early-stage fault prediction. A reduction in the number of trouble tickets, a reduction in the severity of the troubles encountered, the resulting drop in the number of days or hours required to fix a problem, and the ability to direct resources to other functions all have both hard-dollar and soft-dollar impacts.

A service like the NetOps Do-It-Yourself (DIY) will cost a company with 5000 devices (SNMP addresses) just under $1.5 million per year to track. This investment gives regular reports with a view toward anticipating network problems and failures before they happen. Before cringing at the thought of spending $1.5 million, keep in mind several things: This represents a large, mission-critical network. $1.5 million is roughly the equivalent of 8 full-employee cost burdens. That is, it would cost about as much to hire, train, equip, and provide benefits and a travel budget for a group that would chase down problems once they occur. This does not take into account the lost revenues and embarrassment that an investment bank, phone company, or airline would suffer if it lost its network for an hour or two during the typical business day.

Of course, the cost for a smaller network or for a less complete product suite would be significantly less. It all depends on the importance to the bottom line of the network under consideration and the scope of analysis desired.

Justifying the expense should be easy, once management has made the required shift in thinking from tracking down the what, when, where, and why of network failures to looking at a system that can mitigate or avoid such problems altogether.

Look at where your organization is positioned against the other popular management schemes. SNMP has been around for years, and everyone in this industry loves anything with *simple* as its first name. SNMP, however, suffers security concerns which may be even more serious than those of today's Web-based systems. The Web-based Enterprise Management Common Information Model, which lets computers describe and share management information across enterprises, also is on the ascendancy.

From the human resources angle, a Web-based management system can become a kind of electronic leash or electronic prison. There will be no respite from work—even a vacation on the sands of Sanibel Island or an alumni weekend at the old alma mater can be interrupted by a page for help from the net-ops center. While the bad news is that there is no way to hide from work, the good news is that with Web-based access, the problem probably can be resolved in an hour or two without sacrificing an entire week or weekend. Is this good or bad, boon or bane, worthwhile or worthless? The answer (and you read it here first) is an emphatic "yes."

From a practical point of view, there are very few instances in which Web-based network management should be totally ruled out either from a technical or from the human angle. In most cases, Web-based management is a great idea—as long as proper precautions are part of the network planning.

The key area to beware of is *security*. In the next chapter we'll take a look at the security issues that must be dealt with and give some basic ideas on how to deal with the problems of intruders, authentication, and the host of other concerns that must be under control before any network is linked to the outside world.

3

How to Keep Systems Secure

Just as important as being safe on a trip—protecting passports and valuables—is the need to keep a network safe from intruders. Every Web-based management system presents a conundrum to IS planners: How does one manage to provide an open door to the network and, at the same time, keep people out? How secure can an open door be?

Murphy's law says that the worst will happen, so we'll spend a bit of time looking at the disaster recovery aspects of Web-based management in this section.

Before we finish this portion of the trip, we'll stop for a cup of Java. Spending a bit of time in the Java café is important if part of the goal of implementing Web-based management is to bring distributed computing to enterprise applications. Java is the key to implementing this sort of self-service applications. Its cousin, ActiveX, serves much the same function, but due to limits on the scope of this tour, we will focus on Java.

First, however, we'll check into security concerns. If properly executed, a Web-based management system should present no more worries or concerns about security than any other system. Web-based management, as a specific application, poses no more or greater a security issue than allowing Internet access anywhere else in the company. The big *if,* of course, is back in the second sentence—this holds only if the system is properly executed. Allowing Internet access in any network has security issues, but the host of firewalls available on the market today should allow a network manager to address the problem quite well.

The Internet and the World Wide Web are designed to encourage and promote interactivity and information sharing. While network security concerns about using the Internet are real, they certainly are not new.

Just as warnings from your mother about keeping an eye on your suitcase are not unfounded, concerns about intruders are not alarmist nonsense. The Computer Emergency Response Team (CERT) has seen an exponential increase in violation reports, growing from just 130 intrusions in 1990 to 2300 in 1994 to over 10,000 in 1998. CERT's job is to provide a coordinated response to computer security incidents, and it has been busy. The FBI's National Computer Crime Squad is quite concerned that most computer crimes go unreported (in some cases the organization does not know it was hit, in others it wants to avoid the embarrassment of admitting it has a problem). Even with what is reported, the FBI says the annual cost of computer crime is in the multibillion range. This includes everything from actual computer theft to the loss of time and computer services while vandals are poking around networks.

International Data Corporation (IDC) of Framingham, Massachusetts, notes that the misuse of information resources or unauthorized release of proprietary company information are not confined to attacks by outsiders. With increased network access throughout the enterprise, companies must realize that security precautions within the company's internal network can be just as exacting as external security concerns. IP-based communications and networking are part of both the wide area network and the local area network.

At the most basic level, Netscape, Internet Explorer, and other common packages generally have security built into them. For the lowest level of security, this should be enough. But just as no medical emergency is a low-level crisis to the person with the problem, so, too, no IS manager who values having a job is going to look at the network as a throwaway when it comes to security. Just as 100 percent of the patients in a hospital have "the best cardiac surgeon in the city" operating on them (how do the other 99 percent of surgeons make a living?), so, too, most network managers will and should demand the best of security.

Car thieves tend to go after hot, flashy vehicles. (Why tool around in a junker?) So, too, do hackers go after the latest challenges in computing. The area of security is quite important because Web-based management tools are the latest trend in network administration, and almost every large network is somehow connected to the Internet. All of the good things about Web-based management that were discussed in the first two chapters of this book can bounce back and smack you in the face if constant security monitoring is not added to the equation. Remember, if your network administrators can access the network from home, so can the proverbial 14-year-old hacker or the disgruntled employee who is going to rage at the technology that has invaded his life.

This book is not a treatise on network security, and no book will make you an expert in the field. Do consider read-only access as a secure option to allow authorized department managers to see the performance statistics and usage patterns of their corners of the network. Do keep separate parts of the administrative scheme separate. Do change passwords and authorization codes frequently.

Remember that even the most secure government computing environments have been hacked successfully. In fact, concern over security is probably the single most important factor that would negate a corporate move to Web-based management.

There are a host of steps one must take when securing any network environment. Among the key areas to examine are the following:

- Access control
- Authentication
- Encryption
- Connection control
- URL or Java and ActiveX screening
- Monitoring for viruses
- Data privacy
- Auditing site use

All of these areas should be on any security list. There may be many other areas of security concern, depending on the network.

Do not make the mistake of trying to establish a security or access program just for a single use such as Web-based management. All network security should be policy based. And that policy should cover all aspects of network usage, whether it is simple sign-on to the LAN or full System Operator (SYS OP) privileges. If your job function happens to be separate from overall MIS management, check higher up the organization. It is likely that your firm has an IS security program in place and that you can benefit from, or ride piggyback on, that program.

The typical first point of security is a *firewall*. Firewalls usually sit at the primary connection point to an outside network—in this case, the Internet. Some firewall strategies call for isolating or protecting one part of the corporate network from another. By forcing network connections (such as network monitoring, configuring, or other management jobs) to pass through the firewall, they allow security to examine each attempted connection and then to accept or reject the connection based on whatever security policies have been implemented.

Broadly, there are three kinds of firewall architectures: (1) packet header filtering, (2) application-level proxies on gateways, and (3) stateful inspection.

Packet filters typically are implemented at the router level. These filters control both incoming and outgoing network traffic at the packet level. They evaluate the address and application port requested in the packet header. This approach is a low-overhead approach to security and will have little impact on network performance. However, it does not provide true network isolation, so it allows only modest network security.

Application-level proxies on gateways provide much better security. They establish a proxy process on the gateway for each connection requested. Users then interact with the proxy for the application they want to use; in turn, the proxy interacts with the external host on behalf of the user. Note the separation of the two sides of the query—the request is handled at arm's length, allowing good control and true isolation of the network as well as monitoring of each request. There is a price, however. Because both connections and proxies are involved, there is an effective doubling of the gateway processor's load. While proxies are great from a security point of view, the slowing down of the network is apt to upset both the users (who don't care much for security hassles, anyway) and the network administrator.

Stateful inspection provides full network isolation, too. By intercepting packets at the network layer and then analyzing data derived from all seven communication layers in the Open Systems Interconnection (OSI) stack, stateful inspection provides cumulative data against which any communications attempt can be evaluated. It also allows a manager to create a virtual session for tracking connectionless protocols like Remote Procedure Call (RPC)- and User Datagram Protocol (UDP)-based applications. Since proxy processes do not need to be written for each new application or service, this approach can adapt quickly to growing networks.

Disaster Recovery

Implementation of a secure networking program is beyond the scope of this book. However, there is another aspect of security—disaster prevention and recovery—which also should be addressed briefly.

Disaster prevention is the best way to avoid a disaster recovery scenario. Often, being able to monitor a network conveniently from afar will help avoid a disaster recovery operation. Convenient monitoring and reconfiguration will allow the network manager to keep on top of the changing needs of the network, avoiding a crash at inconvenient times (which pretty much means *ever*).

Some disasters are unforeseeable or unavoidable acts of God. But a good Web-based management system, with appropriate security controls, will allow a network manager to work on rerouting or reconfiguring a network that has fallen victim to a natural disaster like a tornado or hurricane. Far from the location that has been affected, the manager can sit at any terminal with Web access, enter appropriate security clearance information, and get into the network to check on the scope of the problem and find out what the situation is before sending a team of technicians to the disaster site, reroute any links that are still functioning, and reconfigure the network to avoid sending any but vital traffic to the office in trouble. All other traffic can be circuited around the down site.

The two most important aspects of this are the first and the last. Even in day-to-day operations, knowing the situation before dispatching help is a major time savings. It also saves frustration on the part of the technician who is charged with the repair. Proper tools; cards, chips, and wire or cable; and even the right personnel will be defined by the Web-based manager before anyone hops into a truck to make repairs.

Rerouting traffic around a troubled site is perhaps the first step that should be taken in any disaster recovery effort. It is the best way to keep a bad situation from getting worse. No matter how vital the location which is affected, not allowing the disaster to spread is of paramount importance. Another key in disaster recovery is prioritizing traffic to or from the site. In many cases, some traffic will be able to get through, albeit at a reduced level. Proper remote reconfiguration of the network (based on priorities established well in advance) will provide vital first aid to a network in trouble.

While it is doubtful that a MIS department will implement the concept of Web-based management predicated on disaster recovery alone, it certainly should be another selling point in any presentation to top management.

Managing the Local Area Network

Probably the best place to start a test program for a Web-based network system is on a corporate local area network (LAN) or on a corporate internal network (intranet).

There are several advantages to starting on an intranet. For one, it is easy to control. It may be that the company even has a testbed network where it tries out software and hardware connections. More typically, there will be a small network whose functions are not vital to the day-to-day mission of the company. It may be a network where the software was written internally or which was designed by internal staff, so knowledge of each nook and cranny is easy to access.

An intranet or LAN is apt to be secure. Many security mistakes or black holes can be identified on the LAN before the problem is rolled out across the entire corporate backbone network.

A LAN can be physically removed both from other internal networks and from the outside world simply by pulling a few plugs. When needed, the connection can be reinstated on one side without involving the other. That is, tests can be run on devices in the LAN from somewhere beyond the corporate headquarters without having any impact on other networks within the corporate firewall.

Start simple. Try to manage one or two devices at most. Look at such issues as connection speed, response time, and the subtle differences one might encounter when working from a laptop rather than a console.

Using a small LAN as a testbed has the advantage of being able to simulate access from miles away while actually sitting next to the devices being managed. All that is required is access to an external host and then access back to the devices or network being managed. No long-distance hassles are involved.

From dealing with a single device on the LAN, the next step would be to deal with a local server. While it might seem a small, insignificant step, in reality it is a giant step because it presents many more management challenges. The range of devices is broader. The need to access and maintain proper device addressing information begins to play a role.

One problem that can be vexing as Web-based management techniques are taken beyond the LAN is the slippage of performance. Any MIS team should anticipate the possibility of a significant difference in performance of the network management system once the operation is taken outside the firewall. It is not a deal killer. But it is something that needs to be anticipated and explained to those who will be using the department's new remote management tools. Be sure to test Web-based access from the most difficult external access points you can find.

Look for software that will reconnect a lost session even if the link is lost during transmission. Anyone who has spent any time trying to access a remote server from an airport phone can confirm that this is a problem that will occur in perhaps one of four calls. Remember, the system is supposed to make life easier for management, not drive the administrators to drink.

Beyond its starring role in the testing stage of developing a Web-based management program, handling the management of most LANs is no different than handling any other portion of the network management scheme.

Managing the Wide Area Network

One of the frequently asked questions about generating Web-based management information from an entire wide area network (WAN) is about the sheer volume of data that is generated. It is logical to think that this information would be a drag on the WAN.

Engineers at NetOps say that's not really the case. While it is true that on a network of 100 targets such an operation will collect gigabytes of data daily, not all of that information is stored. Under a product like their Do-It-Yourself (DIY), or the AT&T Network Solutions package, the data is reduced in two steps. First, multiple thresholds are set for each MIB object monitored. This lets the system determine in real time how severe a result is, without generalizing to a thumbs-up or -down approach. There is no single cutoff for good or bad values; severity talks to ranges of how good or how bad a value is. Once the data is mapped to a severity scale, the program can arrange to store only changes in the event severity (changes in the health) of a given object. If an interface goes down, there is no need to record that it is *still* down every few seconds.

This sort of derivative approach lets the analysis package record the state transition to down and again when it recovers. In short, it provides substantial data compression without the loss of meaningful information. It also allows customization of the thresholds (adapting to baseline normal for a specific environment) and generation of real-time TRAP notification messages when an object changes to the most severe state data reduction.

The lesson to be learned: Save only the meaningful data.

Data is stored in memory and checkpointed to the disk daily. Output files are ASCII and can be parsed with scripts. Some systems Unix-compress the ASCII files when checkpointing and archiving (using a job that also tests for changes in target configuration around midnight). Most Digital Signal Monitors (DSMs) monitor *domains* of roughly 20 to 25 target systems. A typical DSM likely archives about 1 to 1.5 MB of data per day and another 1 MB of configuration information daily.

A Quick Overview of Java

Java is a platform-independent programming language that allows software developers to create one version of an application and deploy it on a wide range of systems. Whether the platform is based on the PC, the Apple Macintosh, OS/2, IBM AS/400, or any of a number of Unix flavors, the Java platform will enable a "Write Once, Run Anywhere" approach to programming.

Java is the product of Sun Microsystems Computer Company, Mountain View, California. If you are familiar with Java, feel free to skip right on to the next chapter. While many readers will probably have done more Java scripting in the past week than the author has in the past year, this chapter is included for those with little or no background in Java computing.

Sun has a description of Java at java.sun.com/doc/general.htm. The Java Web site is key for anyone wanting more information about Java, Java scripting, or an overview of Java. Much of what is in this chapter is based on Sun's documents. While Java's popularity is based largely on its ability to do a job and do it well, it also is the lever being used by a whole multitude of smaller firms who are eager to get their feet into the networking management market. Without something like Java, they would be locked out. Perhaps the best single independent alternative to Java is the Simple Network Management Protocol (SNMP). SNMP is a robust, proven network management vehicle. However, its influence could plateau as vendor-neutral Web-based information becomes a more important part of network management strategies.

Java technologies enable Web-based network management products to deliver real-time network status monitoring, statistics graphs, network discoveries, and problem reports. All of this information is constantly updated and delivered to the client browser automatically. Such is the power and reward of having a Java-based system.

When the shortcomings of traditional architectures—such as Windows95, Windows NT, UNIX, or MacOS—are combined with the existence of interlocking computing environments (that is, the multitude of mainframe, client/server, workstation, and local PC applications), it becomes difficult for an IS department to do an economical job of developing and maintaining systems. Today Java is becoming more and more popular.

Keep in mind, however, that (even in early 1999) it still can properly be termed emerging technology. In fact, it was only introduced in May 1995, so it is really only about four years old—in people years, a mere teenager, even by computing industry standards. However, it promises to mature into a healthy, vibrant adult.

Whether Java becomes the universal operating system, as some pundits feel sure it will, or it does not, the simple fact is that it does an excellent job of bringing distributed computing to enterprise applications. Any time self-service applications are called for, Java should be one of the contenders. When the application becomes complex, the simplest solution probably will be to equip all of the users with one of the several Java-capable browsers on the market and let them surf over on the Web.

Java-based IT architecture consists of several elements (Figure 3.1):

1. A Web server, which serves HTML pages and Java applets to the clients in a corporate intranet, is required. This server may be replicated to increase the number of supported clients without increasing the administrative burden. It may combine the booting service for the thin-client desktops.

2. Distributed application servers are required. On these are kept the business applications or objects accessed by clients across the intranet. Servers can be of any size or performance range, with the choice dictated by the specific application and the department's budget. However, they all will share common features of interfacing with legacy code and databases, and delivering application services to Java clients. The concept of an application server is a logical distinction. In some applications, the application server may be combined with the Web server or applet servers.

3. There will be a number of database, file, mail, print, and directory services and other dedicated servers that must be accessible by Java client applets. Again, some may reside on the same server.

4. Over all of this is needed some sort of integrated management system for managing the servers, networks, and both fat and thin clients. Since we are looking at Web-based network management, this is a good time to let you know that reading this book is putting you on the right track.

Remember that existing legacy systems will have to be integrated onto the network. Some of these will be the traditional fat clients. Others will be thin. But all will have to talk to one another. Java helps make this happen, and also does it in an elegant, but simple, way.

The Java Computing Environment

Available from Sun is a complete set of products and tools for creating Java computing. They are:

- *Java development tools and services.* Products and services to help simplify worldwide development of Java applications.

- *JavaOS.* A highly compact operating system that runs Java applications on devices such as network computers or cellular phones.

- *Java Virtual Machine.* A layer of software, embedded in computer operating systems such as Windows and UNIX, that enables the computer to run Java applications.

- *Java servers.* Server software designed to support Java applications and clients.

- *Java APIs.* Standard software interfaces between Java applications and run-time services such as graphics and networking.

- *Java chips.* A family of microprocessors optimized for Java, enabling even faster performance of Java applications.

- *Java network management.* Java-powered network management tools.

- *Solaris operating system.* A scalable, high-reliability, high-availability, multiprocessor operating system needed to power the servers essential to Java computing.

- *Sun Support Services.* SunSpectrum support for hardware, software, networks and network interoperability products that include Java.

- *Sun Professional Services.* Expert information technology consulting, Internet/intranet practice, educational services, and system integration services for Java computing.

- *Sun Customer Education.* Leading-edge educational services providing Sun-authored Java training for worldwide customers.

Figure 3.1   The Java computing environment.
Source: Sun Microsystems

Java simplifies things in a few different ways. First, its thin clients do not maintain any permanent state. All code, data, and configuration information is stored and managed centrally. This combination of local desktop processing with central management reduces the maintenance cost per seat without sacrificing the ability to customize.

Second, the inclusion of the Java Virtual Machine on the server means that all clients and the server can be programmed as a single homogeneous platform—the Java environment—with consistent tools, training, and documentation.

The Java application development platform provides a portable, interpreted, high-performance, simple, and object-oriented programming language and run-time environment.

In contrast, some management tools, including tools from IBM, offer Web access over the intranet using passive HTML, CGI, JavaScript, VRML, and HTTP. These tools, however, provide access to only static network information. They do not allow administrators to easily view dynamic information or perform real-time management functions through the browser. With Java, network administrators using a simple, Java-capable browser can access real-time information from managed network devices easily and quickly. And Java Web-based network management gives other people within the organization, such as planners and financial analysts, ready access to information otherwise locked in traditional management systems. This information includes statistical data, usage statistics, and billing and accounting information. Through a Java-capable Web browser, this valuable information is available for planning, cost analysis, and cost allocation as well as for network management.

Java Web-based management applications enjoy all the benefits of Java itself. The applications are portable and highly distributable over the network. Because Java applications run on the client machine, the load is reduced on the management application server, increasing the scalability of Java Web-based management solutions. Based on an object-oriented language, IBM's Java Management Applications are highly extensible and robust, making it easy to add new managed resources and devices and new management functionality.

Web-based access ensures that network administrators can access management applications over the intranet from any Java-capable browser and can perform full management functions. No longer are administrators tied to large, costly, specialized network consoles. This will allow organizations more flexibility in the deployment of network administrators and will, ultimately, reduce the cost of network management through better utilization of the administrators and reduced reliance on specialized consoles. For example, if an administrator is responsible for all the routers at a given location, a manager can define a page for him or her that has a hot link to the Nways Workgroup Manager for Windows NT representing each one of the routers.

When contrasted with applications running native code, Java apps are fairly secure. This is because the Java run-time system inspects all applet code for viruses and tampering before running it.

When management applications are written as Java (or ActiveX) components, they can run in the context of an HTML browser. Since we continue to see a blossoming of object-oriented Web development frameworks, ability to customize is becoming simpler and more attractive both to developers and to network managers. If a management application is written in Java and exposes Java classes, those classes can be manipulated with JavaScript. This allows for rather straightforward design and development of custom management applications.

Applications are adaptable to changing environments because users dynamically download application code from anywhere on the network.

Perhaps the key value of Java is the time it cuts out of the applications development process. Because the Java system is easy to test, allows reuse of the same code, and can be deployed via the Internet or a corporate intranet, development and deployment are fast (Figure 3.2). Sun says it figures that up to 80 percent of MIS time and resources are spent maintaining the current set of fat-client applications. Its Java Computing reduces the time spent in developing new business-critical applications. The ability to roll out applications on an intranet Web site allows for much shorter, more iterative application development cycles, quicker debugging time, and less

JAVA APPLETS (SAME APPLETS RUN ACROSS ALL PLATFORMS)	
Java Virtual Machine and Java Classes	**Java Virtual Machine and Classes**
Any Java-enabled browser (e.g., Navigator)	JavaOS
Any OS (Mac, Solaris, Windows, etc.)	Hardware (thin client)
Hardware	
Java "Webtop" on a fat client	Java "Webtop" on a thin client
Applets written in Java run on both fat clients as well as thin clients.	

Figure 3.2   Java applets on fat and thin clients.
Source: Sun Microsystems

frustration in the field. Sun's claims that Java developers see productivity increases of 2 to 5 times over traditional languages such as C or C++ are not far off the mark.

IBM implements its Java Management Application clients as Java applets. Applets can be launched from the topology display on its Nways Manager server without requiring a Web browser. Applets can also be launched remotely by loading a Java Management Application on a Web browser. Any Java-capable browser can dynamically download the management applet into the browser's virtual machine and present the management interface from within the browser's window.

The applet running on the client offloads the management server and provides the user interface as well. It may handle data validation and translation, including internationalization, which allows users in different countries to access the same management application server for the same managed device but view the display in their own language. From the browser, administrators can access real-time information about any given device and perform the full range of management functions that they previously performed from specialized consoles, such as changing a configuration or reassigning ports. The clean separation of the Java Management Application client and server responsibilities allows user interfaces to be designed and enhanced over time without affecting the Java Management Application server.

The Java management server is implemented as a Java application responsible for integration with the rest of the management platform, the creation and maintenance of HTML pages used by remote browsers, and the processing of the bulk of the management application logic. Companies like IBM implement their application logic as a set of objects that provide interfaces to access and control network devices in a protocol-independent way.

Although the device models are protocol independent, they rely on instrumentation objects to translate device information for a specific network management protocol. Currently instrumentation objects have been defined for SNMP, but they can be defined for other protocols as well, IBM says. It is even possible to embed a Java Management Application server in a managed device itself and use instrumentation objects to access its management information locally. Isolating platform dependencies allows the flexibility to integrate the Java Management Application server with other management platforms in the future.

On the other side of the coin is the present cost of hiring a competent Java programmer. In what might be termed "the revenge of the nerds," the ability to put together a respectable Java-based program has become worth big bucks in corporate America. It's great if you're the worker and are looking to buy your next Lexus for cash. It's a major challenge if you're the manager and have to convince the corporate higher-ups that basing your program on Java really is a cost-effective way to run the department.

In building custom software, there are two major concerns: Is the IT team using the best development tools for the job, and will the tools being employed allow integration of the new application into the existing IT architecture? It is crucial when developing Java applets to make sure that they run on multiple browsers and Java device platforms. This ensures that there is no inadvertent dependency on any nonstandard application programming interfaces (APIs).

The essence of Java computing is a client/server model in which Java application code is dynamically downloaded from server to client on demand. In some cases, the applets are stored in cache on a hard disk at the client location. In other cases, the applets are stored only in dynamic RAM (DRAM). Because applications normally reside on a server and are delivered to the client only when called for, administration can focus on the central server. Further, this assures that all users are accessing the latest application release level made to the server (and not each individual client). In addition, there is no need for local administration of AUTOEXEC.BAT, WIN.INI, SYSTEM.INI, PROTOCOL.INI, or any of the other configuration files in use.

As an open, standards-based approach, Java Web-based management will allow organizations to leverage their existing investments in hardware, platforms, and associated training while they benefit from freedom of choice in their management platform and workstation operating system decisions in the future. This will enable organizations to reduce both hardware and administrative network operations costs.

Until Java Web-based network management, managing corporate networks presented several difficult and costly challenges. Often administrators had to use a different, specialized console for each management application. As a result, organizations had to invest in costly hardware and management platforms. Administrators needed extensive training in the use of each specialized management tool, and they could not easily perform other management chores without additional training. As corporate networks grew, the number of administrators required and their deployment became a serious problem.

IBM says its Java Web-based management meets these challenges, delivering the following benefits in the process:

- *Reduced need for large, central management servers and specialized consoles.* By downloading functionality to the administrator's

Java-capable browser, the client workstation running a simple, Java-capable browser is able to take over a portion of the processing chores previously performed exclusively by the management server and specialized consoles.

- *Reduced training.* Java-capable browsers provide a simple, consistent user interface to all management applications, allowing administrators to quickly transfer their knowledge of network management from one application to another.

- *Flexible, efficient deployment of administrators.* With the ability to access management applications and data from any client machine on the network running a Java-capable browser, administrators can be deployed where they are most needed. They are not tied to a particular management console.

- *Leveraging of management information.* Through the use of Java-capable browsers, others within the organization have access to network management information for such purposes as planning, business analysis, and cost allocation.

Java applets can run anywhere. Sun has heavily promoted the idea of *Java Virtual Machine* software. It assures that Java applets can run in any Java-enabled browser (including, of course, Netscape Navigator and Microsoft Internet Explorer). This allows a gradual migration to a simple-to-manage client: the Java device. This is a desktop client machine that is connected to the network and can download and run any Java applet, but is free of the complexity and client administration needs of a traditional PC. So, rather than a traditional operating system (OS), the Java device contains a JavaOS with a Java Virtual Machine. Both can be stored at the client in flash ROM or can be booted from the network. Client data storage is done centrally on the file server.

Applets running on the client communicate with servers via standard network protocols. A Java client may open a standard TCP/IP socket connection with an application server. There are literally dozens of vendors who serve the intranet market for switches, routers, hubs, and the other boxes necessary to set up a TCP/IP network.

Alternatively, more sophisticated client/server protocols can be employed. The Java Database Connectivity (JDBC) protocol provides Structured Query Language (SQL) connectivity to databases. More complex, three-tiered applications can be built using distributed objects with industry-standard Common Object Request Broker Architecture (CORBA) protocols. Three-tiered or multitiered application models are the key to leveraging existing back-end systems.

A company like IBM has as its stated overall goal to create an effective network computing infrastructure robust enough to support reliable, high-volume electronic business. To achieve this goal the strategy is to make Java the industry-standard server platform, with its capabilities accessed via standard protocols and the JavaBeans standard component interface. To exploit this server platform IBM uses Java Web-based clients and servers that can download management application functionality as needed and take over management functions from the central management server.

This downloading, or offloading, of functionality improves scalability by reducing demand for computing resources (storage, memory, and processing) on a management server. Offloading these views to clients enables each server to handle many more devices, which reduces the need for more or larger central management servers as the network grows.

When selecting a Java development tool, there are three primary criteria: (1) application type, (2) developer platform, and (3) developer experience. For example, professional developers with C or C++ experience who need to build a high-performance, complex Online Transaction Processing (OLTP) application should look at integrated Java development environments like Sun's Java WorkShop. Web developers with HTML experience who need to create animated Web pages might want to consider tools like DimensionX Liquid Motion. Commercial designers and developers without much programming experience can look at tools like NetDynamics from Spider Technologies or Infospace's WebSeQuel. There are a host of other good products out there, as well.

Java can be used to access existing database and transaction systems as well as for new business applications. Sun has extended Java to connect to databases, through the JDBC Java database API; to CORBA-based object servers, through a Java/IDL API; and to other object servers, through a JavaBeans API (this integrates Java, ActiveX, OpenDoc, and Live Connect objects into a cross-platform framework). In addition, many of Sun's Java partners have developed other useful connectivity tools, such as Open Connect's Web Connect 3270 emulator written in Java.

Future enhancements to Java's toolset should offer many growth and expansion opportunities in areas that are ticklish today. Java security enhancements are intended to permit the Java Management Application client to safely operate outside the Java sandbox and become more autonomous from Java Management servers. With JavaBeans, programmers can create reusable parts, which customers and third-party developers can use in visual application builders. This will increase the rate at which new management programs for specialized devices come to market.

It will also allow customers to adapt commercial components to their networking needs. This will add further value to every compatible product on the market.

One final consideration must be dealt with when dealing with Java: Are its most ardent supporters really Java fans, or are they really Microsoft haters who will do almost anything and deal with anyone that promises to free them from Microsoft technology? A good argument can be made that Java is an easy sell to the anti-Microsoft legions. And there is plenty of truth to that argument.

Still, Java has the potential to be a real star. Just be sure to weigh the pros and cons before betting the farm on Java's potential. It's growth and progress to date have been phenomenal. If it continues, making a small investment in Java today will pay off handsomely tomorrow. Yet, the computer software world is notorious for chewing up and spitting out wonderful programs (who uses WordStar or Lotus 1-2-3 anymore?).

At least in the world of Web-based network management, the IS department that moves into the Java realm is going to have a lot of company. Many, many vendor firms are heavily committed to Java. Every one of their existing and future customers is likewise committed to Java. If there is safety in numbers, Java is looking safer every day.

Take a look at the next chapter and see how many of the commercial products listed are tied to Java or are migrating in the direction of Java. So, we'll continue our tour of Web-based network management with a look at who is doing what in the world of commercial Web-based management systems.

Who's Doing What
with Web-Based Systems

There are at least a couple of dozen vendors who offer products for Web-based network management. Some work on proprietary systems. Others will work with a variety of vendors' products. If it's time for your company to start sending out Requests for Proposals (RFPs), this list is the place to start.

The setup on each vendor's product is nearly identical. There is contact information with Web address, fax number, and phone number (toll-free numbers generally will work only in North America or inside the United States, so a standard number also is provided).

In every case, the vendor was contacted and asked to provide a standard suite of information. Almost all replied promptly. Their data is included here. The varying lengths of the product descriptions is not meant to signify any discrimination as to quality or value of the product. It simply means that some product managers provided a bit more detail than did others. The descriptions are merely intended to help provide a list of potentially useful products and to help readers sort out those that appear to be appropriate before going through the bid or purchase process.

The information is as complete and accurate as possible at the time this book was written. To obtain the most current information on each vendor product, please access the URL given for each of the 30 vendors listed; also feel free to contact the author at curt@curtharler.com. The accompanying chart (Figure 4.1) summarizes the various products, but for the best feel for any given product, refer to the full description.

Checking Versions

The current version is one of the more important sections to check. Products that are in 1.0 are new to the market. The upside is that they are likely built on the latest technology, focus on a market niche that the developer saw was not being served, and are more likely to be flexible on price and more eager to do business to get some cash flowing in the door. The downside is that the product, which likely has gone through extensive beta testing, has not seen the field use that a product in version 1.2 or 1.3 has seen.

Usually manufacturers who have made minor improvements on a software package give their products "dot upgrades," raising the version from 1.2 to 1.3. When major changes or significant new features are added to a software package, the manufacturer changes the entire version, perhaps from 2.4 to 3.0. The good news with products in later versions is that they usually are well field tested. The kinks have been worked out. Even a product with a version like 3.0 or 4.0 is likely to be substantially field proven, although there may still be some rough spots in the latest part of the package. If the newest features are important to you, it might be better to wait for version 4.1—just to let someone else take care of finding the bugs. Some of the products have user groups—a sort of professional club that focuses on that particular package. Those user groups can be more valuable in a pinch than the company's own engineers. They are less likely to be blinded by the religious fervor which some engineers bring to their jobs.

The downside to purchasing a higher-version package is that you may be buying a lot more functionality than you really need and that will have an effect on the bottom line. Some established vendors realize that and offer product pricing on an à la carte basis. There is likely to be less price flexibility (if that is a consideration in your purchasing matrix). As a purchaser, you are more likely to be one fish in a sea of customers—rather than a key customer that the vendor would like to use as a reference in building its customer base.

Some of the buying decision will depend on how computer-literate you are or how much you and the others on your staff are inclined to tweak a product. If you are looking for a plug-and-play solution, the more mature products are probably going to be more to your liking. Should the plug not play, there are going to be a lot more people out there who can help you out.

Contacting Vendors

In most cases where a firm is building a case to move to Web-based network management, the first step is to ask for a Request for Proposal (RFP) or Request for Quotation (RFQ). The easiest place to find a host of good companies is on the chart in Figure 4.1 which accompanies this chapter. You may want to photocopy the chart for your internal use and use the Web addresses listed to request information from the vendor. Read through the in-depth product descriptions that follow and eliminate those products that obviously do not fit your requirements. Then compose a simple message to the vendors left on the list, telling them that you are considering a move to Web-based network management, and include a brief description of your computing environment. That should elicit a prompt response. "Prompt," in my experience, ranges anywhere from under two hours to over a month. More typical was the overnight to two-day response. Be sure to give the vendors a valid, live address for responses so that responses are not misrouted and do not sit unnoticed in someone's in-box for days.

It is a good idea when building an RFP to leave a number of open-ended areas. Unless you have absolutely hard-and-fast requirements delineating every detail of what you expect the network to require, it is best to leave some gray or fuzzy areas in the request. Most of the sales engineers working for vendor companies have seen many more networks (both well-planned, successful ones and ones that would be appropriate on midnight horror movies) than has the typical manager just getting into the area of Web-based network management. Leave room for their ideas and concepts. While a network manager, ethically, should really be shopping for a Web-based management system, by using the open-ended RFP strategy it is possible, in effect, to obtain free information from several expert consultants. They may come up with ideas or strategies never considered in any of your organization's meetings. Do not be surprised if the solutions presented in response to such an RFP leans heavily on the company's product. However, by cross-referencing several of the proposals, it should be possible to come up with a good idea of what professional experts feel would be most suitable for your network.

Overview of Vendors

VENDOR NAME	PRODUCT NAME	RELEASE VERSION	JAVA-ENABLED?	WEB ADDRESS
3Com, Inc.	Transcend Traffix Manager for Windows NT	2.0	Yes	www.3com.com
ARESCOM, Inc.	Remote Manager	3.0	NA	www.arescom.com
Asanté Technologies, Inc.	IntraSpection	1.0	Yes	www.asante.com
AT&T Solutions	Global Enterprise Management System (GEMS)	7.1	Not for Java network connections, but is capable of Java scripting	www.att.com/solutions
Bay Networks, Inc.	Optivity Network Management System	8.1	Yes	www.baynetworks.com
Boole & Babbage, Inc.	Explorer family	1.0	Yes	www.boole.com
Cabletron Systems	SPECTRUM Enterprise Manager	5.0.1	Yes	www.cabletron.com
Candle Corp.	ETEWatch	1.0	Java compatible	www.candle.com
Computer Associates International, Inc.	Unicenter TNG	2.2	Does Java scripting and VRML	www.cai.com
Concord Communications, Inc.	Network Health	4.0	Yes	www.concord.com
Edge Technologies, Inc.	edge N-Vision	2.01	Yes	www.edge-technologies.com
Extreme Networks	ExtremeWare Enterprise Manager	2.0	Yes	www.extremenetworks.com
FastLane Technologies, Inc.	Virtual Administrator for Windows NT	2.0	Yes	www.fastlanetech.com
Fujitsu Network Communications, Inc.	Speedport FENS-AN	1.0	Yes.	www.fnc.fujitsu.com
Hewlett-Packard Co.	HP TopTools HP BenLink XL Software	4.1 1.3	Yes ActiveX	www.hp.com/toptools www.hp.com

Figure 4.1 Overview of Web-based network management vendors.

Overview of Vendors (Continued)

VENDOR NAME	PRODUCT NAME	RELEASE VERSION	JAVA-ENABLED?	WEB ADDRESS
IBM Corp.	Nways Workgroup Manager	1.1	Yes	www.networking.ibm.com
INRANGE Technologies Corp.	INTERVIEW *DataWizard*	2.0	No	www.inrange.com
Jyra Research, Inc.	Service Management Architecture	2.0	Yes	www.jyra.com
Micromuse, Inc.	Netcool Suite	3.3	Yes	www.micromuse.com
NetOps Corp.	Do-It-Yourself (DIY) Network Analysis	2.0	Yes	www.netops.com
NetScout Systems, Inc.	NetScout Manager Plus NetScout AppScout NetScout WebCast	5.2 1.0 1.1	No Yes Yes	www.netscout.com
Network Associates, Inc.	Sniffer Service Desk	2.0	No	www.nai.com
Novadigm, Inc.	Radia Software Manager	2.0	Yes	www.novadigm.com
Novazen, Inc.	Interactive Customer Care	1.0	Yes	www.novazen.com
Phasecom, Inc.	CyberManage for SpeedDemon	1.0	Yes	www.speed-demon.com
Pinnacle Software Corp.	Axis Web	1.0	Yes	www.pinnsoft.com
Sterling Software, Inc.	SOLVE:Netmaster for TCP/IP	4.0	Java scripts only	www.solve.sterling.com
Telco Research Corp.	TRU Enterprise Network Accountant	1.0	Java based	www.telcoresearch.com
Tivoli Systems, Inc.	Distributed Monitoring	3.6	Yes	www.tivoli.com
Wipro Corp.	CyberManage	3.0	Yes	www.wipro.com
Xedia Corp.	Access Point	1.5	Yes	www.xedia.com

Figure 4.1 Overview of Web-based network management vendors.

Contrarian Thinking

There is a contrarian bid analysis process which might be good to keep in the back of your mind when looking at proposals. It holds that the top bidder or the top proposal is actually way out of line—the company either is trying to sell one of everything or simply is trying to make a lot of money because it suspects you are a babe in the woods. At the other end of the scale is the low-cost, bare-bones proposal. It is unlikely that such bidders understand the full impact and scope of what you are requesting; or, it is likely that they are trying to get a foot in the door and up-sell you on the other components that should be included in the original offer. Look at the great mass of proposals (or at least the several bids) that fall in the middle range. These vendors most likely understand what it is you are looking for. Of course, there will be variations in the specifics of what they propose. Some may toe the line of exactly what you mentioned in your RFP. Others may show you ideas which may or may not work. They should not be penalized for ideas that you deem are not appropriate right away—at least they are thinking and are demonstrating their willingness to help you succeed with the new venture. Cull the ideas that your team feels are irrelevant. Keep the good ones. Winnow down the number of vendors who are asked for final proposals. Include the best points from all. You eventually may need to go through a Value-Added Reseller (VAR) or distributor who works with several vendor companies to get all of the features you feel are necessary to implement a successful Web-based management system.

Going through the process actually should be fun. While it probably will not have the excitement of snowboarding at Aspen or sailing on the lake, it will be educational. By the time you've finished this book, and re-reviewed this chapter, you will be prepared to go one-on-one with the vendors listed. In every case, their engineering and support staff is knowledgeable and helpful.

Now, turn the pages and see what kinds of Web-based network management goodies await.

3Com, Incorporated

Santa Clara, CA
Southborough, MA
Tel: 408-764-5000
www.3com.com/products/trans_net_man.html

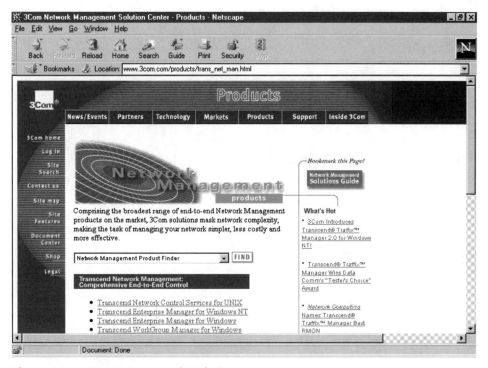

Figure 4.2   3Com, Incorporated, Web site.

Product Name:

Transcend Traffix Manager for Windows NT

Current Version:

2.0

Operating System Compatibility:

Windows NT

Browser Compatibility:

Internet Explorer 3.0 and above
Netscape Navigator 3.01 and above

Java Enabled?

Yes

Systems Compatibility:

Windows NT Server

Product Vis-à-Vis RMON:

Supports RMON2

Suggested Applications and Important Information:

Transcend Traffix Manager 2.0 for Windows NT offers Web-based reporting, efficient data storage and retrieval, and comprehensive RMON2 data collection capabilities. These enhancements provide administrators with more insight into network traffic flow, application usage, and end-user activities, giving them powerful resources to better manage network operations.

Transcend Traffix Manager 2.0 for Windows NT offers a choice of HTML, ASCII, and printed report formats to simplify the sharing of information, provide for customized reports, and enable the export of data to other applications. A scheduler function, new in version 2.0, allows for report generation on a daily, weekly, or monthly basis, and user-defined data aging maximizes storage space for past performance data. The latest version also doubles the number of supported end nodes—from 50,000 to more than 100,000—and incorporates an open database to allow access to information by third-party applications.

Transcend Traffix Manager provides a desktop-to-WAN visualization of enterprise traffic to help network managers better understand the impact of application deployment throughout the network. Transcend Traffix Manager collects and correlates data, providing a global view of network traffic for performance management, trend analysis, and troubleshooting. Through its GUI, it can quickly and easily drill down to every host and data stream in the network, allowing managers to monitor and enforce corporate network usage policies.

The package scales from small to large enterprises. Administrators can use Transcend Traffix Manager to aggregate subnet data from many devices into a single device. In addition, it can filter out conversations below a level defined by the user, providing a more useful set of information.

Transcend Traffix Manager 2.0 shipped in the fall of 1998. The U.S. list price is $7995. Customers who already had purchased Transcend Traffix Manager V1.1 for NT and have software maintenance contracts are eligible to receive an upgrade free of charge.

ARESCOM, Incorporated

Fremont, CA
Tel: 510-445-3638
Fax: 510-445-3636
www.arescom.com

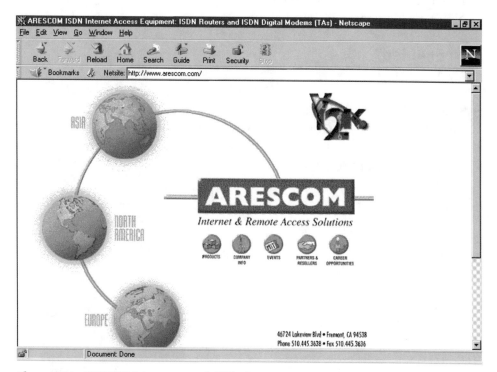

Figure 4.3   ARESCOM, Incorporated, Web site.

Product Name:

Remote Manager

Current Version:

3.0

Operating System Compatibility:

Works only with the Apex Manager 4.0, which was released late in 1998.

Browser Compatibility:

Internet Explorer 3.0 and above
Netscape Navigator 3.01 and above

Java Enabled?

N/A

Systems Compatibility:

Works with the ARESCOM Apex product line.

Product Vis-à-Vis RMON:

Not RMON enabled

Suggested Applications and Important Information:

The Remote Manager software for the Apex 1100 ISDN BRI router lets network managers and Internet service providers (ISPs) optimize network performance and resources. It complements the Apex Manager's capabilities, letting management install, monitor, troubleshoot, and maintain ISDN connections. It comes with comprehensive diagnostic capabilities, which operate with an intuitive GUI or command line administration via telenet or local console.

Remote Manager supports 16 connection profiles, providing a flexible array of dial-in and dial-out combinations including caller ID block to prevent unwanted calls, faxes, or errant dial-ins. Networking enhancements include port mapping for Internet traffic associated with particular ports, routing information protocol (RIP) for faster route setup, proxy arp for faster connection setup, and dial-on-demand routing, letting the user dial any one of multiple locations depending on profile setup. It lets the Apex 1100 connect simultaneously to two separate locations through MultiConnect or SplitB. This eliminates the need for two Apex routers on the same LAN. It supports 16 IP filters, increasing security available for restricting network access. Best of all, it was available free—at least until the end of 1998—to all comers with the Apex Manager 4.0.

Asanté Technologies, Incorporated

San Jose, CA
Tel: 800-662-9686; 408-435-8388
Fax: 408-432-7511
www.asante.com

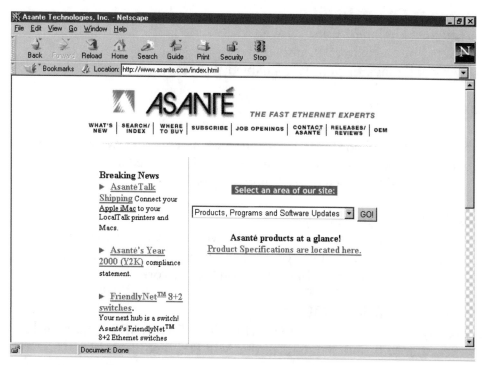

Figure 4.4 Asanté Technologies, Incorporated, Web site.

Product Name:

IntraSpection

Current Version:

1.0

Operating System Compatibility:

Asanté Fast 100 Hub
3Com LinkSwitch 1000 Ethernet switch
Bay Networks 2800 stackable 10 BASE-T hub

Browser Compatibility:

Internet Explorer 3.0 and above
Netscape Navigator 3.01 and above
Any other JavaScript or Java-enabled Web browser

Java Enabled?

Yes. Java technology enables this product to deliver real-time network status monitoring, statistical graphs and tables, network discoveries, and problem reports that can be continually updated and automatically delivered to the network manager.

Systems Compatibility:

Requires an NT-based Web server. However, product is platform-independent and can be used with any Web browser, on any client (Windows NT, Unix, or Macintosh) on the network.

Product Vis-à-Vis RMON:

Compliant with RMON MIB specifications, SNMP, MIB II, Standard Repeater MIB, and Standard Bridge MIB Ethernet-like MIB.

Suggested Applications and Important Information:

IntraSpection claims to be the first SNMP management product based entirely on intranet technology, a technology that is being widely and rapidly adopted. Designed to run on your Web server, it provides network management capabilities for an entire network anytime, anywhere there is WWW access. IntraSpection allows network managers to locate, correct, and track network problems from any client on the network equipped with a Web browser. The network manager loads the software on a Windows NT–based workstation. When a network device experiences a problem, it sends an error message to the IntraSpection Trap Manager, which captures and logs the problem through a Windows-based OBDC database interface. The network manager can access the error log and view system events via any off-the-shelf, SQL-based database, from any client, regardless of whether it's on the network or an independent device. IntraSpection tracks the "health history" of the network, providing the network manager with a comprehensive, historical record of network problems and resolutions.

It allows users to develop a customized device management system using HTML, unlike other solutions that require knowledge of C and C++ languages, as well as SNMP programming. Customers can create their own management modules with IntraSpection or use the Personality modules offered by the vendor, which have the same look and feel and feature extensions that were previously available only with vendors' proprietary network management packages.

Network administrators can manage the entire network through a standards-based network management foundation. IntraSpection is compliant with SNMP, MIB II, Standard Repeater MIB, and Standard Bridge MIB. Its Map Manager function instantly builds and displays a map of the network and incorporates changes, deletions, and additions to the network as needed. Network functions can be displayed in graphical or tabular form.

The basic IntraSpection software is available to download from the Asanté Web site. Documentation, service and support are be provided separately and will be priced at $295.

Personality Modules are list priced at $99 per module. The first three modules available will support the Asanté Fast 100 Hub, 3Com's Link-Switch 1000, and Bay Network's 2800. The company promises availability of additional modules. The Vendor Pack, a bundle of vendor-specific device Personality Modules, is list priced at $795. The company plans to make available Advanced SNMP modules, which perform sophisticated network management tasks.

AT&T Solutions

Florham Park, NJ
Tel: 973-443-2100
www.att.com/solutions

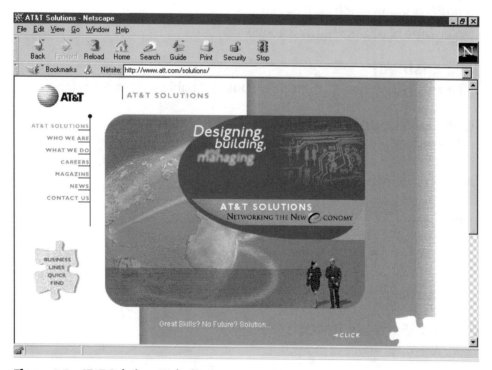

Figure 4.5   AT&T Solutions Web site.

Product Name:

Global Enterprise Management System (GEMS)

Current Version:

7.1

Operating System Compatibility:

Sun Solaris 2.4, 2.5.1, 2.6

Hewlett-Packard UX 10.01, 10.10, 10.20, 11.0

Browser Compatibility:

Internet Explorer 4.0 and above

Netscape Navigator 4.0 and above

Java Enabled?

Not for Java network connections but is capable of Java scripting.

Protocol Support:

The system is built for use with AT&T's system only.

Systems Compatibility:

HP Overview

N-Vision

EPRO

Concord

Remedy ticketing

Crystal Reports

Product Vis-à-Vis RMON:

N/A

Suggested Applications and Important Information:

The key focus of AT&T Solutions' Global Enterprise Management System (GEMS) is to predict network failures before they occur. With its latest release of the sophisticated proprietary software platform, AT&T Solutions has continued to improve the networking management performance of a product first introduced in 1995, allowing it to solve problems significantly faster for clients whose local and wide area networks are managed from the vendor's Global Client Support Center. Release 7.1 of the platform produces seamless networking management capabilities by integrating proprietary software developed at AT&T Labs with best-in-class enterprise management software, including products from Microsoft, Hewlett-Packard, Memco, Remedy, Oracle, and other major vendors.

The GEMS platform integrates best-in-class people, processes, and tools. It is modular, scalable, and deployed globally through AT&T network support centers located in the United States, Canada, United Kingdom, the Netherlands, India, China, and Singapore.

GEMS 7.1 runs more than 100 different applications and 250,000 lines of "gluecode" on more than 100 servers for clients of AT&T Solutions' outsourcing and outtasking services. It is an agile and flexible platform capable of rapid customization without compromising quality or reliability. To accommodate upgrades seamlessly, critical pieces of the GEMS platform can be "hot swapped" without impact on service to customers. The new platform release gives clients Web-based access to a suite of client support services as well real-time disaster recovery and backup, network intrusion protections, and an interface to the rest of AT&T's systems and applications.

GEMS 7.1 builds upon the performance monitoring and predictive management capabilities of earlier releases and supports the full range of enhancements to AT&T Solutions' suite of managed offerings, including AT&T Network Analysis Services for wide area network support, and AT&T WorldNet Managed Firewall Service.

Additional enhancements implemented in the GEMS 7.1 release include the following:

- Improvements in trouble ticket reporting
- Addition of a capability for notifying multiple people in multiple locations for predictive, proactive, and reactive network management
- Real-time replication of ticketing and critical business data for disaster recovery and backup
- Detection of attempts at intrusion into clients' networks, plus security audit reporting
- Tighter electronic bonding to the gateways of the AT&T's Worldwide Intelligent Network

The end-to-end management capabilities of GEMS 7.1 span a broad range of applications and devices involved in clients' networks, including PCs, servers, PBXs, LANs/WANs, hub switches, routers, frame relay access devices (FRADs), digital service units (DSUs), and multiplexers. The vendor targeted the platform to be fully "Year 2000" compliant by year-end 1998.

Bay Networks, Incorporated

Santa Clara, CA
Billerica, MA
Tel: 800-8-BAYNET
Fax: 978-916-4102
www.baynetworks.com

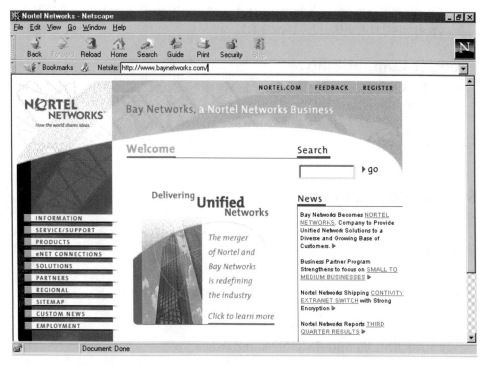

Figure 4.6   Bay Networks, Incorporated, Web site.

Product Name:
Optivity Network Management System

Current Version:
8.1

Operating System Compatibility:
Solstice Domanager Manager 2.3 under Solaris 2.5 or 2.5.1.
SunOS support has been discontinued with release 8.1.
HP OpenView Network Node Manager v4.1, 4.11, 5.0.1.
Tivoli TME10 NetView for AIX 4.1.
NetArchitect supports Ethernet and ATM only with Centillion MCP
versions 2.0.4, 2.0.5, 2.1.0 or 2.1.1.

Browser Compatibility:
Internet Explorer 3.0 and above
Netscape Navigator 3.01 and above

Java Enabled?
Yes

Systems Compatibility:
HP UX 10.1 or 10.2
HP UX 9.x support discontinued with the current release
AIX 4.1 or 4.2
Bay Networks Agents
Windows NT (under Optivity Analysis for Windows NT)

Product Vis-à-Vis RMON:
Supports RMON and RMON2 standards

Suggested Applications and Important Information:

The Bay Networks Optivity suite covers a broad range of products. Included are Optivity LAN, for local area networks and switched internetworks; Optivity Internetwork, a management solution for router and remote access systems; NETarchitect, a policy-based configuration suite for switched internetworks; and Optivity Web, the company's Web-based tool for managing Bay Networks routers. It is the latter that is of most interest here.

Optivity Web is a suite of tools from the Optivity NMS applications. It has been Web-enhanced to provide state-of-the-art features for fault and performance management of switched internetworks. The product's HTML-driven Web pages deliver Web-based, forms-oriented router management, providing fault and performance status information. A network manager can track and diagnose anomalies in the router network and drill down to investigate router configuration data or protocol behavior.

The company's OmniView performance and diagnostic monitoring product has been enhanced to support Centillion ATM LAN Emulation statistics. This is in addition to its current capability to show performance and diagnostic information on Ethernet, Token Ring, and ATM ports or bridge groups.

The network manager is presented with a quick view of performance and error characteristics of any networking device in real time.

Bay purchased Netsation, developer of a Web-based management product called Network Configurator, in February 1998.

Boole & Babbage, Incorporated

San Jose, CA
Tel: 408-526-3000
Fax: 408-526-3053
www.boole.com

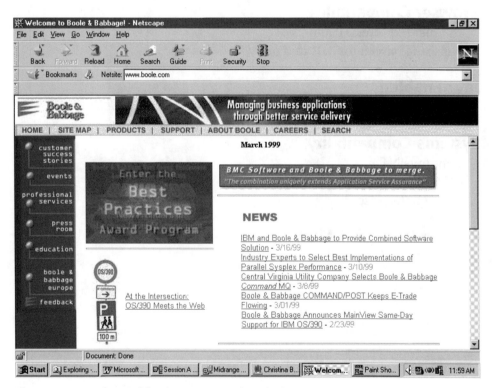

Figure 4.7   Boole & Babbage, Incorporated, Web site.

Product Name:
Explorer family

Current Version:
1.0

Operating System Compatibility:
Any Windows-NT based PC
MAX/Enterprise Unix servers

Browser Compatibility:
Internet Explorer 3.0 and above
Netscape Navigator 3.01 and above

Java Enabled?
Yes

Systems Compatibility:
Windows NT
COMMAND/Post
MAX/Enterprise

Product Vis-à-Vis RMON:
N/A

Suggested Applications and Important Information:

The major component in the Explorer family is the COMMAND/Post Explorer. It includes a full-featured enterprise service-level management console built on Windows NT technology. It integrates organizationwide event information with new policy-based criteria and supports existing COMMAND/Post and MAX/Enterprise servers.

The system has graphical, textual, and multimedia representations of business-critical services, simplifying the process of monitoring and managing enterprise availability. From any Web browser or Windows NT–based PC, a broad base of corporate users can access and manage the entire IT topology or specified parts of it—from a business service view down to the individual node.

COMMAND/Post Explorer is based on ActiveX technology and fully supports Microsoft's Distributed Component Object Model (DCOM). The interface is quite intuitive and allows users to simplify and customize management views based on their specific needs and responsibilities. For example, IT managers may define domains that are meaningful to a particular end user, such as a CIO interested in high-level business service views, or an operator needing to access native system consoles to take corrective action from the desktop. This also reduces the total number of alarms an operator must consider, streamlining management to find and correct the root cause of problems.

Video and 3-D capabilities greatly expand the possibilities of storing information needed in the operations management process.

Tight integration with Microsoft Office applications is provided with a direct interface to Excel for real-time and historical graphical reporting. ActiveX and DCOM support also allows standards-based data access to any OLE- and ODBC-compliant databases or applications.

The product is available for both COMMAND/Post and MAX/Enterprise users. Pricing ranges from $750 to $5000, according to configuration. The company indicates that volume discounts are available.

Cabletron Systems

Rochester, NH
Tel: 603-332-9400
www.cabletron.com

Figure 4.8   Cabletron Systems Web site.

Product Name:

SPECTRUM Enterprise Manager

Current Version:

5.0.1

Operating System Compatibility:

Microsoft Windows NT 4.0
Sun Solaris 2.5.1, 2.6
Unix

Browser Compatibility:

Internet Explorer 3.0 and above
Netscape Navigator 3.01 and above

Java Enabled?

Yes

Systems Compatibility:

Microsoft Windows NT 4.0; OS service patches will be identified as
they become available.
Solaris 2.5.1, 2.6
OpenWindows 3.5.1 and CDE 1.0.2 for Solaris 2.5.1
OpenWindows 3.6 and CDE 1.2 for Solaris 2.6

Product Vis-à-Vis RMON:

SPECTRUM is RMON enabled.

Suggested Applications and Important Information:

The SPECTRUM Enterprise manager is part of a new series of advanced applications targeted at the service-level management marketplace. New capabilities in this latest version include the following:

- A Service-Level Management Solutions Map across multivendor application, computing, and networking requirements

- New solutions for combining business-process and service-level management

- Significant advances in service-level management for ISP wide area network environments

- A new family of multivendor switched administration applications to build a foundation for service-level management in the switched network environment

- Enhancements in fault resolution, change management, and new Java-based autodiscovery

- Integration of clearVISN V2.2 for real-time management and load-balancing across devices from the Digital Network Products Group (DNPG), a unit of Cabletron

The product allows easier synchronization of IP addresses. Users can schedule periodic synchronization of network node names within the Domain Naming System (DNS) and the Network Information Service (NIS) with their SPECTRUM model counterparts. This automated process eliminates the potentially error-prone chore of updating both databases. The Web Alarm view, an HTML Web-based application, has been improved to include Event information, model-specific information (such as location, contact person, and device notes), and more detailed Probable Cause/Status information, with a link to pertinent information about the device on which the alarm is occurring. The Event Log provides improved event data access through a defined start-and-end time range of events. Also, an improved column listing allows the user to view event information (such as Date/Time, Model Name, Model Type, Event Code, User Name, and Event Message) by event categories. Improved Event sorting and searching allows users to quickly list and find events. Improved filtering, searching, table function, navigation from model-based events, and preference setting all increase Event Log usability.

The SPECTRUM 5.0 family of products introduces a Service-Level Management Solutions Map that addresses the three key SLM environments: (1) applications level, (2) computing level, and (3) transport level. These solutions leverage SPECTRUM's advanced technology for fault resolution and real-time IS administration, as well as SPECTRUM's strengths in providing cohesive management across switched and traditional networks, systems, and applications.

SPECTRUM on NT is not a scaled down version of SPECTRUM, or a 16-bit product for NT. SPECTRUM on NT is the same 32-bit application that has achieved success on UNIX. SPECTRUM 5.0 on NT is completely interoperable with SPECTRUM 5.0 clients and servers executing on Unix platforms. All applications now have the look and feel of the Windows NT 4.0 platform.

New to 5.0 is RingView, an add-on application that provides the same support for Token Ring networks that is provided by the RingView for FDDI application. Features include ring performance, topology automapping, token order, and fault isolation.

Enterprise Configuration Manager (ECM) for SPECTRUM centralizes control of device configurations throughout the enterprise. Through new, powerful, easy-to-use interfaces, generic configurations can be created for a class of devices. With a simple command, ECM upgrades firmware for thousands of switches, or adjusts configurations for thousands of routers based on time-of-day requirements. Configurations can also be cut and pasted from one model to another, and stored for reconfiguration purposes for disaster recovery.

SPECTRUM 5.0 includes a number of significant enhancements for fault resolution. Topping the list is new spreadsheet functionality for Enterprise Alarm Manager and new Case-Based Libraries for SpectroRX. SpectroRX is a dynamic problem-solving tool that customizes solutions based on individual case histories. There also is a new Java-based Automated Discovery and Modeling System (ADaMS) released first as a stand-alone tool that will translate IT assets into easy-to-read spreadsheet groupings for flexible, comprehensive updates. In the future, ADaMS will provide intelligent modeling and topology that will integrate with SPECTRUM Enterprise Manager.

Candle Corporation

Santa Monica, CA
Tel: 800-972-2635; 310-829-5800
www.candle.com

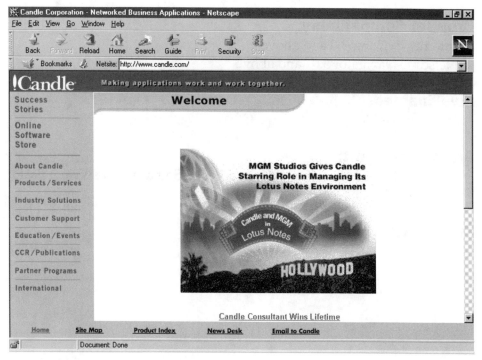

Figure 4.9   Candle Corporation Web site.

Product Name:
ETEWatch for Browsers
ETEWatch for Networked Applications

Current Version:
1.0

Operating System Compatibility:
Windows NT 4.0
Windows95
Unix

Browser Compatibility:
Internet Explorer 3.0 and above
Netscape Navigator 3.01 and above

Java Enabled?
Java compatible

Protocol Support:
Supports Lotus Notes, SAP R/3, and PeopleSoft as well as Visual Basic, PowerBuilder, and C++

Product Vis-à-Vis RMON:
N/A

Suggested Applications and Important Information:

The ETEWatch family provides end-to-end application response time monitoring from the perspective of the end user, not network elements. It measures the time it takes a transaction to complete a round trip, from the moment it starts and as it crosses the network, to the servers, and back to the desktop. ETEWatch lets a network manager look at the applications total performance for a single user, a group of users, or the entire enterprise.

It can send application response-time information and alerts to framework software like HP OpenView, CA's Unicenter, or Tivoli TME 10. All monitoring is nonintrusive. Response-time data (to the millisecond) is collected by the program agents, which reside on a desktop machine. Data is transmitted to a server where a corporate or departmental database can be maintained. The product tracks everything from mouse clicks to page scrolls and screen choices to show how the intranet or Internet sites are being used. It is not fooled by terminated browser requests, Java animations, or other applets that continue to send and receive data after a transaction is completed.

Pricing starts at $1495 and varies depending on the customer's configuration.

Computer Associates International, Incorporated

Islandia, NY
Tel: 516-DIAL-CAI
Fax: 516-342-4295 (PR Department)
www.cai.com

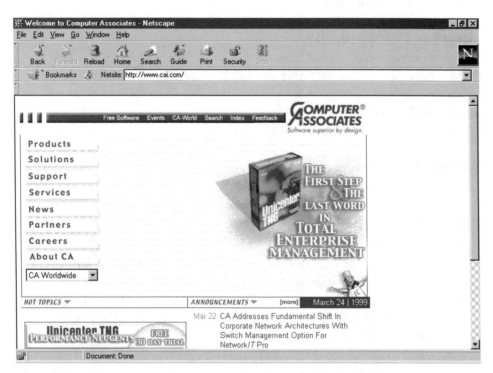

Figure 4.10   Computer Associates International, Incorporated, Web site.

Product Name:

Unicenter TNG

Current Version:

2.2

Operating System Compatibility:

Unix—30+ platforms
Windows NT
Tandem NSK
IBM AS/400 plus other proprietary OSs
OS/390 compatibility

Browser Compatibility:

Internet Explorer 3.0 and above
Netscape Navigator 3.01 and above

Java Enabled?

Does Java scripting and VRML

Protocol Support:

IP, IPX, SNA, and DECNET

Product Vis-à-Vis RMON:

Product supports both RMON1 and RMON2. Unlike RMON
monitoring systems that deal only with RMON1/RMON2, Unicenter
TNG brings its full range of management capabilities to bear for
RMON environments, systems using MIB/MIB2, and those IT assets
using WBEM. Unicenter TNG's object model supersets these
standards, therefore enabling it to flexibly manage virtually all IT
assets and even nontraditional IT assets (i.e., utility meters, oil rigs,
refrigeration systems, etc.).

Suggested Applications and Important Information:

Unicenter TNG is an integrated enterprise management solution that enables organizations to manage all IT resources, encompassing heterogeneous networks, systems, applications, and databases. It provides comprehensive end-to-end enterprise management. According to the manufacturer, Unicenter TNG is the only fully integrated management solution covering network discovery, topology, performance, events and status, security, software distribution, storage, workload, help desk, change management, and other functions for traditional and distributed computing environments, as well as for the Internet and intranets. Unicenter TNG's intelligent manager/agent technology delivers highly scalable management of the entire computing environment, including hardware and software.

The TNG Real World Interface allows global network administrators to use their Web browsers to obtain a three-dimensional view of their network. The TNG Interface uses Virtual Reality Markup Language (VRML) in the same way a Web browser uses Hypertext Markup Language (HTML). Those VRML files give a three-dimensional view of the network that allows the administrator to inspect, navigate through, and interact with the devices throughout the network in a way similar to playing a video game.

A number of Microsoft products have been brought under the Unicenter management umbrella. Included are ISS, transaction server, message queuing server, SQL server, exchange server, and outlook.

CA's solutions provide access control, authentication, and authorization for complete and unified cross-platform security. This enables organizations to set security policies that map directly to business objectives. These solutions even secure Web servers, allowing organizations to exploit this dynamic resource with confidence. Through an integrated set of core services such as scheduling, workload management, event correlation and console management, output management, and problem management, CA solutions enable organizations to automate mundane administration tasks. These capabilities bring an unprecedented level of automation to distributed environments.

This lets a firm manage its networks as an interdependent extension of other business-critical resources. These solutions cross traditional network boundaries by managing all industry-standard network protocols, such as TCP/IP, IPX, SNA, and DECnet. They enable administrators to centrally manage their network assets as an integrated part of their enterprise.

The Desktops and Servers product suite lets organizations manage desktop and server resources as an integral part of the enterprisewide environment. Highly scaleable, these solutions provide cradle-to-grave control, managing everything from setup to ongoing operations to asset tracking.

The application management solutions use a common set of services for all applications. Through comprehensive and integrated Web server management, these solutions enable organizations to confidently exploit the Internet, intranet, and extranet to their fullest extent. They help management ensure Web site availability and manage business-critical Web resources to provide ongoing security and availability. These capabilities deliver ongoing security and integrity to a Web environment.

Concord Communications, Incorporated

Marlboro, MA
Tel: 800-851-8725; 508-460-4646
Fax: 508-481-9772
www.concord.com

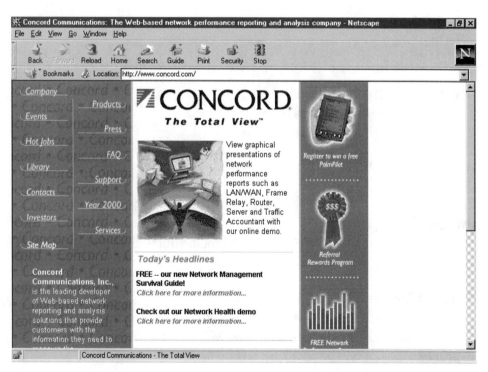

Figure 4.11   Concord Communications, Incorporated, Web site.

Product Name:

Network Health

Current Version:

4.0

Operating System Compatibility:

Works under UNIX, with a Sun SPARCstation or compatible clone, or
HP 9000 Series 700 and 800 or compatible clone
Solaris 1.1.2 (Sun OS 4.1.4), 2.5.1, 2.6
HP UX 9.07, 10.20
Open Windows
OSF/Motif
CDE
SNMP

Browser Compatibility:

Internet Explorer 3.0 and above
Netscape Navigator 3.01 and above

Java Enabled?

Yes

Protocol Support:

Supports all major network protocols, including SNMP and the RMON
suites.

Product Vis-à-Vis RMON:

Supports RMON1 and RMON2 (requires 0.6 MB free disk space for
each polled statistical element and 30 MB for each polled RMON2
probe).

Suggested Applications and Important Information:

Network Health is a family of Web-based software applications that automatically collects, analyzes, and presents critical network performance patterns in an easy-to-read, graphical format. It automatically reports back to the network manager and covers virtually every crucial area of the network, from the backbone devices like hubs, routers, and frame-relay circuits to the servers running specialized applications support functions. Powerful grouping capabilities let IS mangers define reports for specific subsections of the network. This allows matching reports to particular teams, departments, divisions, or geographic areas.

The program gives a service-level view of the enterprise, allowing network managers to understand network performance, optimize existing resources, and plan for the future.

Network Health leverages existing network hardware by talking to the MIBs already embedded in these devices. The software intelligently pulls only the key variables needed to analyze and report on the network—generating virtually no network polling traffic that could impact network performance. It automatically discovers network devices, collects data, and intelligently presents it in graphic form.

Concord has partnerships with most major network hardware providers, including Bay Networks, Cabletron, Cascade, Cisco, Hewlett-Packard, NetScout, Newbridge Networks, Sun Microsystems, and Xyplex. Its products support moderate-sized networks all the way up to the world's largest organizations in monitoring tens of thousands of elements. Information is gathered from the elements and presented in a single, easy-to-read panel that can be used by executives at all levels of the organization.

Add-on modules allow network managers to extend functionality and expand coverage as needs or budget allow. The family includes ATM, frame relay, LAN/WAN, remote access, router/switch, server, service-level reporting, and traffic accountant modules.

Network Health relies on an SNMP poller that collects data from installed routers, hubs, and RMON agents with minimal effect on the network. Pricing starts in the area of $15,000 to $20,000 and includes the cost of a software console with the Web interface, and grouping and scheduling capabilities, as well as the reports and the integrated database. Additional segments and RMON2 probes cost extra.

Edge Technologies, Incorporated

Fairfax, VA
Tel: 703 691-7900 ext 226
Fax: 703 691-4020
www.edge-technologies.com

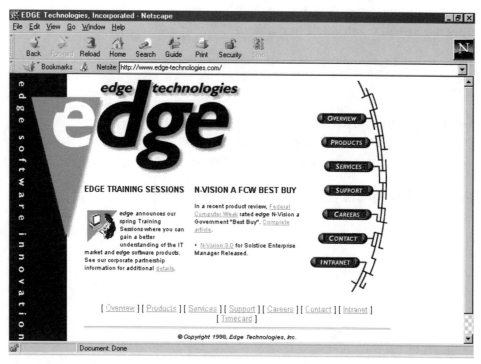

Figure 4.12   Edge Technologies, Incorporated, Web site.

Product Name:
 edge N-Vision

Current Version:
 2.01

Operating System Compatibility:
 Sun Solaris 2.4, 2.5.1, 2.6
 Hewlett-Packard UX 10.01, 10.10, 10.20, 11.0

Browser Compatibility:
 Internet Explorer 3.0 and above
 Netscape Navigator 3.01 and above

Java Enabled?
 Yes

Systems Compatibility:
 HP Network Node Manager version 4.x, 5.x
 Solstice (Domain, Sunnet, and Site) Manager 2.2.3

Product Vis-à-Vis RMON:
 N/A

Suggested Applications and Important Information:

The edge N-Vision product is primarily a remote network management tool. It provides real-time access to network information via any Java-enabled Web browser.

N-Vision does require a Java-enabled Web browser on Windows NT, Windows95, or on a Unix-based platform.

A look at the rough pricing for the product puts a concurrent 5-user license at about $15,000. The fee for a 10-user license is $20,000, and for a 20-user concurrent license, $50,000. An unlimited site license would have a list price of $75,000.

Extreme Networks

Cupertino, CA
Tel: 888-257-3000; 408-342-0999
Fax: 408-342-0990
www.extremenetworks.com

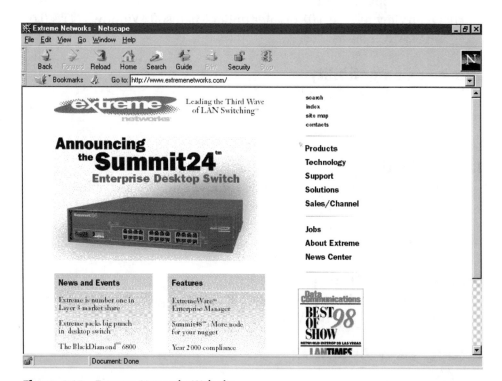

Figure 4.13   Extreme Networks Web site.

Source: © 1999 Extreme Networks. All rights reserved. Extreme Networks, ExtremeWare, ExtremeWorks, ExtremeAssist, PartnerAssist, Extreme Standby Router Protocol, ESRP, Leading the Third Wave of LAN Switching, BlackDiamond, SmartTraps, Summit, Summit1, Summit4, Summit4/FX, Summit24, Summit48, Summit Virtual Chassis, SummitLink, SummitGbX, SummitRPS and the Extreme Networks logo are trademarks of Extreme Networks. The Extreme Turbodrive logo is a service mark of Extreme Networks. All other trademarks and service marks are property of their respective owners. Specifications are subject to change without notice.

Product Name:

ExtremeWare Enterprise Manager

Current Version:

2.0

Operating System Compatibility:

Microsoft Windows NT 4.0 running on an Intel platform

Sun SPARC Solaris 2.5.1

HP OpenView release 5.01 or later under Microsoft Windows NT 4.0 or
Sun SPARC Solaris

Browser Compatibility:

Internet Explorer 4.0.1 and above

Netscape Navigator 4.0 and above

Or any browser that supports Java 1.1

Java Enabled?

Yes. Client applications can be accessed using any Java-enabled
browser. These Java applets can be downloaded from the server to a
client machine on request, and executed in a Java-enabled Web
browser that supports Java 1.1.

Systems Compatibility:

The ExtremeWare Enterprise Manager can manage Summit switches
that are running ExtremeWare 2.0.

Product Vis-à-Vis RMON:

N/A

Suggested Applications and Important Information:

ExtremeWare Enterprise Manager is a powerful yet easy-to-use application suite that makes it easier to manage a network of Summit switches. Virtual LANs (VLANs) and policy-based Quality of Service (QoS) can be set across the network where enterprisewide management is a given. This product is based on the Sun Java Web Server. The server is responsible for downloading applets, running servlets, managing security, and communicating with the database. A relational database management system (RDBMS), Sybase SQL Anywhere, is used as both a persistent data store and a data cache. ExtremeWare Enterprise Manager Server supports Login security and enables the manager to grant different levels of user access to specific application features. It integrates with HP OpenView, and can be launched from within the HP OpenView Network Node Manager application.

The QoS feature of Summit switches lets managers set different service levels for outbound traffic. Using QoS, you can specify the service that a traffic type receives. QoS Manager lets you create, modify, and delete custom QoS profiles that are available to all Summit switches known to the database. These profiles can be applied as QoS policies for any VLAN. Users with Manager-level access can use the Inventory Manager to add or delete switches from the database. They can also refresh the information in the database about any or all switches under Enterprise Manager control. Once a switch is "known," or added to the Enterprise Manager database, it can be managed by the VLAN Manager, Virtual Chassis Stack Manager, and the QoS Manager.

The Inventory Manager keeps configuration and status information obtained from the switches it manages. Basic status information is updated through periodic polling. Any changes to switch configuration data made through ExtremeWare Vista, the ExtremeWare command-line interface (CLI) or another SNMP management process cause the switch to generate SmartTraps. To avoid the overhead of frequent polling, the SmartTraps are used to identify changes in switch status and configuration. The Enterprise database is then updated, which eliminates the need for frequent, detailed polling. Inventory Manager also provides a *sync* operation. This operation obtains status information from the switch on demand if the user feels switch configuration information is not being correctly reported in the Enterprise Manager applets. Whenever a status or configuration change occurs, ExtremeWare software in a switch uses the SmartTraps rules to determine if the Enterprise Manager should be notified. This can be triggered by changes in switch status, such as fan failure or overheating, or configuration changes made on the switch through the ExtremeWare CLI or ExtremeWare Vista. Every five minutes, Enterprise Manager also performs a default "heartbeat" check of all the switches it is managing to determine if they are still accessible. In addition, the ExtremeWare Enterprise Manager offers the ability to explicitly gather switch status at any time using the sync command from the Inventory Manager applet.

ExtremeWare Enterprise Manager also provides software to launch the Enterprise Manager client from within HP OpenView, either from the Tools menu or from a pop-up menu from the Network Node manager map.

FastLane Technologies, Incorporated

Halifax, Nova Scotia
Tel: 800-947-6752
www.fastlanetech.com

Figure 4.14   FastLane Technologies, Incorporated, Web site.

Product Name:

Virtual Administrator for Windows NT

Current Version:

2.0.

A new product, DM/Administrator 4.0, is being released. The new
version will offer added features such as Virtual Administrator 4.0,
with Active Directory simulator.

Operating System Compatibility:

Windows NT 4.0, NT 3.51.

Domain model can be imported to Active Directory when Windows
NT Server 5.0 is deployed.

Browser Compatibility:

Internet Explorer 3.0 and above

Netscape Navigator 3.01 and above

Java Enabled?

Yes

Systems Compatibility:

Virtual Administrator 4.0 provides both a network client (standard
Win32) and a Web client.

Product Vis-à-Vis RMON:

N/A

Suggested Applications and Important Information:

FastLane's Virtual Administrator provides a network client and a platform-independent Web client for delegated administration tasks. Virtual Administrator for Windows NT delivers the power to delegate administrative rights within a domain or across multiple domains. It allows administrators to delegate simple, repetitive tasks to non-NT administrators or virtual administrators, who can perform specific, authorized functions, improving the efficiency of network administration and enforcing effective security policies.

There is no limit to the granularity of granting user rights, and strong security can be implemented by granting only the appropriate rights. This allows Windows NT network administrators to delegate high-frequency, low-complexity tasks and remain focused on more critical network tasks. The virtual domains created by Virtual Administrator are secure and do not change the physical domain structure of Windows NT.

Virtual Administrator provides a platform-independent Web-browser-based GUI for remote virtual administration. Virtual Administrator 4.0 provides a hierarchical virtual domain structure that allows for creation of an NT 5.0-like directory structure on NT 4.0. With Windows NT 5.0 and Active Directory support, Virtual Administrator's administrative structure will be able to shelter users and virtual administrators from changes in the physical domain structure of enterprise networks. The product includes an Active Directory simulator, allowing enterprises to deploy hierarchical domain architecture on Windows NT Server 4.0 to test or modify a functional hierarchical domain model prior to the release of Active Directory. This domain model can be imported to Active Directory when Windows NT Server 5.0 is installed.

Virtual Administrator 4.0 will provide delegation of printer and share management in addition to user and group management. The virtual domains created by Virtual Administrator are secure and do not change the physical domain structure of Windows NT Server.

North American pricing begins at $7 (U.S.) per managed user, with site license pricing available for larger installations.

Fujitsu Network Communications, Incorporated

Richardson, TX
Tel: 800-777-FAST (3278)
Fax: 972-479-6990
www.fnc.fujitsu.com

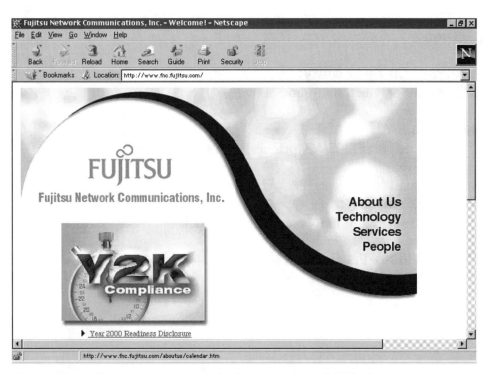

Figure 4.15   Fujitsu Network Communications, Incorporated, Web site.

Product Name:

Speedport FENS-AN

Current Version:

1.0

Operating System Compatibility:

Works in a Solaris environment with a Sun Enterprise 450 server.
Solaris 2.6 (5/98)
OpenWindows
OSF/Motif
CDE
SNMP

Browser Compatibility:

Netscape Navigator 4.04 and above

Java Enabled?

Yes. Speedport FENS-AN primarily uses Java Scripting along with
some Java.

Protocol Support:

Complies with the TMN model at the EML level

Product Vis-à-Vis RMON:

Not RMON enabled

Suggested Applications and Important Information:

Speedport FENS-AN is a Web-based element management system for Fujitsu's ADSL equipment. It was primarily designed to support the access network using SNMP for monitoring and provisioning. The first release is dedicated to supporting the Fujitsu/Orckit Speedport ADSL product line with full monitoring and provisioning capabilities via user-intuitive GUIs. FENS-AN provides equipment and service provisioning, alarm monitoring, and software download through an easy-to-use HTML browser interface. The server requires Solaris 2.6 and communicates with the hardware via SNMP. The server will initially support up to 100,000 ADSL lines and 30 concurrent users in the first release. FENS-AN uses HTML tables for the shelf indication. This arrangement is effective for remote users because it requires little to be downloaded to the browser other than the HTML page itself. Colored table cells indicate alarm severity and are hyperlinks to a description of the alarm type and possible causes.

The network elements are arranged according to user-specified logical groups, which can be used to designate central office (CO), state, or regional groupings. A tree widget is included to allow the user to quickly and effectively navigate to the network element and open the applicable display. FENS also monitors all incoming alarms from the shelves and will indicate to the user the alarm type and location. If more information is required, the user is able to drill down to a full description of the alarm and a list of possible causes. One of the most powerful features this product offers is the ease with which the user can provision customer ADSL circuits. The GUI provides a flowthrough of the entire ADSL circuit from the Frame Relay concentrator to the ADSL modem in the customer's home. Any problems with the circuit will appear on this screen in the form of alarm indicators. The system indicates alarms ranging from failed frame relay circuits all the way down to a 10BASE-T link failure in the customer's home. It is also possible to view circuit statistics such as current line rate, line attenuation, and maximum potential line rate. All circuits can be uniquely identified with freeform text dialogs, as can the Frame Relay circuit itself. This capability provides the user with a powerful tool to add any information about the customer that may be appropriate—from name and number to past troubles.

Hewlett-Packard Company

Palo Alto, CA
Tel: 800-752-0900; 970-635-1000
Fax: 800-231-9300
www.hp.com/toptools

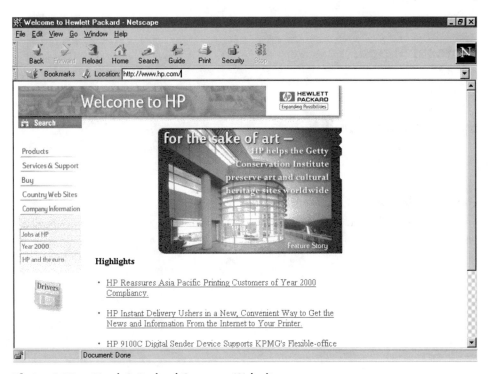

Figure 4.16a   Hewlett-Packard Company Web site.

Product Name:

HP Top Tools

Current Version:

4.1

Browser Compatibility:

Internet Explorer 4.0 and above
Netscape Navigator 4.0 and above

Java Enabled?

Yes

Protocol Support:

DMI
SNMP

Systems Compatibility:

HP OpenView
Microsoft-SMS

Product Vis-à-Vis RMON:

Supports SNMP and RMON

Suggested Applications and Important Information:

HP TopTools is a Web-based management software application that manages multiple standards-based PC devices, allows access from multiple operating systems, and plugs into industry-leading network management systems. This application is the first of several initiatives aimed at simplifying the three-tiered hardware, management software, and network-management system structure of a typical enterprise, leading to what HP believes will be an increasingly self-managed PC environment.

The new HP TopTools Web-based management application, by being better able to source a hardware problem, will offer faster remote administration and increased hardware availability. The use of a single point of entry to manage most LAN-based PC devices will reduce the learning time required for performing management tasks. It also will eliminate the need for a dedicated management console, making any PC with a Web browser the management console, anywhere. Eventually, the vision for this product is an expectation that the need for onsite visits to repair PC hardware will be eliminated—reducing lost time and money in terms of unproductive time by the user or MIS staff.

Expanding on HP TopTools PC management software for HP Vectra commercial PCs and HP Kayak PC Workstations, this product enables configuration, administration, and monitoring of HP NetServer systems, HP Omnibook notebook PCs, HP palmtop PCs, HP AdvanceStack Hubs and Switches, and other networked devices from one easy-to-use application.

The new HP TopTools Web-based management application also will continue to manage all standards-based networked devices—not just HP products—maintaining HP's commitment to open, standards-based management solutions. The TopTools Web-based management application will support device management standards, such as DMI and SNMP.

In the future, HP says it expects to offer a range of manageable DMI attributes built directly into the hardware of its full line of HP Vectra commercial PCs, HP Kayak PC Workstations, HP NetServer systems, HP Omnibook notebook PCs, HP palmtop PCs, HP AdvanceStack Hubs and Switches, and other networked devices. These attributes will offer a host of new hardware diagnostics, trouble-shooting, and self-healing capabilities that will ease setup and deployment.

Hewlett-Packard Company

Palo Alto, CA
Tel: 800-452-4844 X-6292
970-635-1000
Fax: 800-231-9300
www.hp.com

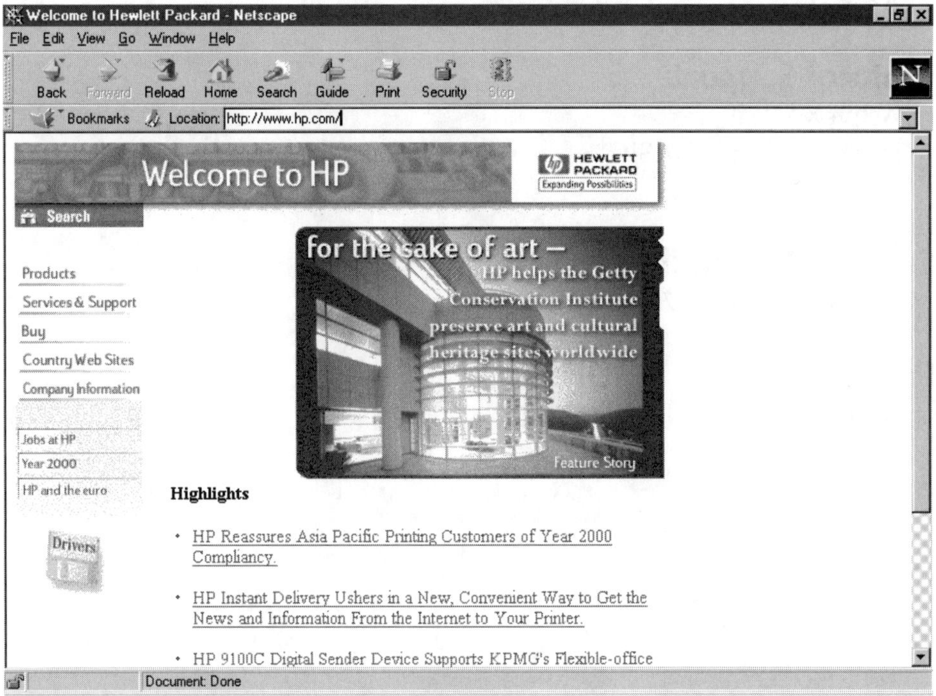

Figure 4.16b   Hewlett-Packard Company Web site.

Product Name:
HP BenchLink XL Software

Current Version:
1.3

Browser Compatibility:
Internet Explorer 4.0 and above
Netscape Navigator 4.0 and above

Java Enabled?
ActiveX

Protocol Support:
ActiveX
Microsoft Visual BASIC
Visual C++

Systems Compatibility:
HP 16600A and 16700A Remote Logic Analyzers

Product Vis-à-Vis RMON:
N/A

Suggested Applications and Important Information:

The HP 16600A and 16700A are the first Web-enabled remote logic analyzers and are among the first of the completely Web-enabled instruments. This capability allows users to access an HP logic analyzer from anywhere, whether over the Internet or through a corporate intranet.

Available in the second quarter of 1999, the system uses HP BenchLink XL software to let PC users easily export data over a LAN from an HP logic analyzer to a Microsoft Excel spreadsheet, simply by clicking an icon in the Excel toolbar. Users can also program the logic analyzer with custom applications or test suites.

Web-enabled control allows users to check the status of a logic analysis session without being anywhere near the analyzer. For example, long-duration measurements set up in a lab can be monitored from a home PC overnight or on weekends. The Web-enabled logic analyzer technology gives full access to all analyzer controls from browsers. It provides users with unparalleled flexibility in configuring and running measurement systems remotely.

The software is available at no charge to registered users of the 16600A/700A series analyzers. HP says it expects to add support for other software applications in the future.

IBM Corporation

Research Triangle Park, NC
Tel: 800-426-2255
www.networking.ibm.com

Figure 4.17   IBM Corporation Web site.

Product Name:
Nways Workgroup Manager

Current Version:
1.1

Operating System Compatibility:
Windows NT
AIX

Browser Compatibility:
Internet Explorer 3.0 and above
Netscape Navigator 3.01 and above

Java Enabled?
Yes. IBM claims to have more Java developers at work than Sun, itself, does.

Protocol Support:
Passive HTML
CGI
JavaScript
VRML
HTTP

Product Vis-à-Vis RMON:
Supports both RMON and RMON2 with embedded agents

Suggested Applications and Important Information:

The current enhanced version of Nways Workgroup Manager for Windows NT and the Nways Manager for AIX extend IBM's Java Web-based management to include Java Performance Management. Java Performance Management is a distributed, flexible, integrated and open set of functions designed to enable performance monitoring of any of the Java-based device managers.

This allows users to create and view performance graphs and reports in any one of several formats, for IBM and non-IBM networking devices; receive notification when performance thresholds are exceeded or when a potentially unfavorable performance trend is occurring; generate stand-alone, dynamically updateable reports that are accessible from any Java-enabled Web browser; and analyze historical performance data for network planning and fault prevention.

Users who might benefit from this functionality include help-desk and network-support personnel, network operators, data analysts, and managers.

The Nways Workgroup Manager for Windows NT and Nways Manager for AIX products represent the beginning of a comprehensive Java-based network management vision for IBM. IBM's strategy encompasses enterprise WANs (Nways Enterprise Manager). Under this strategy the Enterprise Manager would provide support for the management and configuration of emulated LANs (ELANs), virtual LANs (VLANs) and switched broadband networks, such as ATM and frame relay. Ultimately all Nways management products will be Java-based, making them portable to any platform running a Java Virtual Machine (JVM), distributable over the network and accessible via any Java-compliant Web browser.

Although the scope of the management function for the first release of the Nways Manager products focused on device management, the product architecture provides a solid base for expanding that functionality to embrace higher-level management application functions. These include topology, fault, performance, configuration, and operations management.

The IBM strategy is to distribute data collection and as much management application processing as possible by extending the DPM function beyond gathering performance data only. Initially, data collection and processing will be distributed to objects running on servers near network devices. Over time the data collection and processing can be distributed to any managed device that runs a JVM, resulting in a truly scalable management solution.

Security issues with Web access are handled at a number of levels. Local access to the Nways Manager servers and the Java Management Application functions is controlled by the operating system's own security functions, which include user accounts, passwords, file and directory protection, and registry protection. Remote clients access the Nways Manager HTML pages and Java code only through a Web server, which provides its own security to a greater or lesser degree depending upon the specific Web server and the security options that administrators choose to implement. For minimal security, Web servers should be configured to control access based on client IP address/hostname and user id/password challenges. The Java Management Application also supports HTTPS, the secure version of HTTP that provides Secure Socket Layer (SSL) protection. This protection includes safeguards against eavesdropping, modification and playback attacks, and impersonation attacks. The Java applet, unlike an ActiveX component (which is not used in Nways), is designed to run only within a restricted area, called the *sandbox,* where it is isolated from the client platform. The Java applet also is unable to communicate with any other host except that from which it was downloaded. As a result an applet would not damage the local system or the Java application server. And network management typically takes place behind the firewall to prevent outside clients from sending requests to servers on the inside, adding another level of security.

The efforts of IBM's Networking Hardware Division (NHD) are coordinated with the work of Tivoli, an IBM company that provides system management applications and platforms for comprehensive integrated network and system management. At the low end NHD introduced Nways Workgroup Manager for Windows NT, which included NHD's first implementation of Java technology. The Workgroup Manager supports networks of up to 200 network nodes. For larger networks NHD offers its campus solutions, which run on either the Tivoli TME 10 NetView or the HP OpenView platform.

INRANGE Technologies Corporation

Mount Laurel, NJ
Tel: 609-234-7900
Fax: 609-778-8700
www.inrange.com

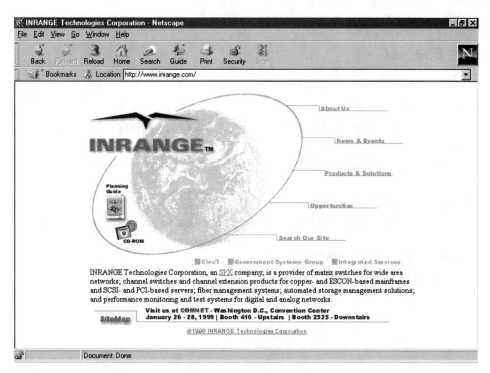

Figure 4.18 INRANGE Technologies Corporation Web site.

Product Name:

INTERVIEW *Data Wizard*

Current Version:

2.0

Operating System Compatibility:

Windows95, NT 4.0
INTERVIEW O/S 14.02 (proprietary)

Browser Compatibility:

None

Java Enabled?

No

Protocol Support:

Frame Relay: Encapsulates PPP, IP, TCP, and other data protocols.
ISDN: Encapsulates PPP, IP, TCP, and other data protocols.
PPP: Encapsulates IP, TCP, and other data protocols.

Systems Compatibility:

Compatibility with INTERVIEW protocol analyzer and Windows PCs

Product Vis-à-Vis RMON:

No RMON capability

Suggested Applications and Important Information:

The INTERVIEW *DataWizard* software allows a PC to remotely control one or more INTERVIEW sessions using a LAN or Internet facilities. It also allows more than one PC to remotely analyze data collected in real time from an INTERVIEW protocol analyzer/emulator at the same time. It is specifically designed for Windows95/Windows NT 4.0 and features setup dialog boxes, tabbed configuration forms, pull-down menus, and icon-based toolbars. This software can be used to operate resident programs on the INTERVIEW via the PC, to transfer complied programs from the PC to the remote unit, and to capture the data stream from the remote unit to the PC for real-time decoding and analysis.

Software applications support Frame Relay, ISDN, PPP, SNA, and X.25 protocols, as well as many data protocols such as IP and TCP encapsulated in the protocols previously mentioned.

This product is useful for the remote monitoring of "dark site" data centers. It is also useful for the mobile field service technician, because the real-time access is provided via the Internet. In addition, it can be used for analysis sharing between distributed network operators, because the real-time data can be viewed by several operators at the same time, located anywhere in the world.

Jyra Research, Incorporated

San Jose, CA
Tel: 408-954-7394
Fax: 408-432-7235
www.jyra.com

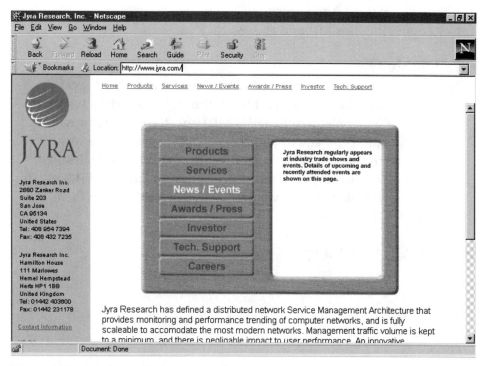

Figure 4.19   Jyra Research, Incorporated, Web site.

Product Name:

Service Management Architecture (SMA)

Current Version:

2.0

Operating System Compatibility:

Windows NT 4.0 with Service Pack 3 and later
UNIX Solaris 2.5.x and later

Browser Compatibility:

Internet Explorer 3.0 and above
Netscape Navigator 3.01 and above

Java Enabled?

Yes. The product is closely linked with Web server technology. The
configuration of the system is achieved through interaction with a
Java-based GUI applet within an HTML page. Reports are provided as
HTML tables and embedded Java graphs. Summary reports are
exported by the management-level manager (MLM), while detailed
reports are exported by the remote service-level managers (SLMs). This
ensures that detailed data traverses the network only when there are
specific HTML requests for it.

Systems Compatibility:

HP UX
IBM AIX/MVS
HP/MPE ix
Windows NT
Novell

Protocol Support:

As over 98 percent of the SLM's code is written in Java, it is relatively easy to port it to any platform that supports the Java Virtual Machine and permits network layer access to the Operating System TCP/IP communications stack.

Product Vis-à-Vis RMON:

N/A

Suggested Applications and Important Information:

Jyra Research has defined a distributed network management, the Jyra Service Management Architecture (Jyra SMA), architecture that will accommodate large volumes of management traffic and the scale of modern networks without impacting user response times. The Jyra architecture incorporates a resilient, reliable, distributed, data collection system that does not impact user traffic and that directly measures application response times; a distributed analysis capability that allows for variable values to be monitored networkwide and for sophisticated analysis to be carried out at remote locations—that is, without transporting large files back to the management center for analysis; and browser-based access to networkwide statistics from any point in the network.

Jyra's Service Management Architecture (SMA) measures quality of service delivered to the desktop user connected to large corporate networks or the Internet. SMA offers Web reports on the performance and latency of a network by monitoring the flow of each application's traffic along its entire length or path.

The key features distinguishing SMA from its competitors are the active Java agents and the distributed data collection and reporting, and its flexible container structure, which permits a hierarchy of collection and reporting formats that are limited only by the discretion of the administrator—functionally, those "containers" (folders or directories) enable collections and reports to reflect logical groupings, geographies, or organizational requirements. SMA is scalable to large networks because of the distributed database for response-time collection, the centralized management and configuration, and the ability to import network topologies from HP OpenView or comma delimited network data files.

Data analysis is performed by the MLM and presented through the automatic generation of summary reports. Response-time traps assist in problem resolution by highlighting locations where degraded response times are occurring. The combination of application response-time data and intermediate router round-trip delay data also assists in isolating whether performance issues are network- or client/server-related. The study of response-time reports can assist in medium- to long-term architecture planning by highlighting trends in response times from multiple network locations.

The application response-time traps support the near-real-time monitoring of the end-user experience of application performance, providing direct problem reporting. SLA reporting is achieved by the summary reports providing actual response times against predefined SLA thresholds. Management reports are automatically generated as aggregated summaries of location and/or application server-specific response-time data. The aggregation rules followed in the generation of these management reports can be defined in terms of the underlying business relationships between each client population and its associated application servers.

Performance testing and tuning can be supported by deploying Jyra SLMs in a preproduction test environment and configuring specific polling tasks. The generated reports will provide valuable data on the application performance in relation to the test network. And, Web development is specifically supported by its HTTP polling capabilities.

The performance and analysis capabilities of the Jyra SLA detailed here feed directly into network performance and trend analysis decisions. Network capacity decisions can be made by reference to the response-time trends over time illustrated in the summary and detail reports. It also provides a direct method of measuring response-time SLA performance from the end-user perspective, providing the monitoring component of service-level management.

Micromuse, Incorporated

San Francisco, CA 94107
Tel: 415-538-9090
Fax: 415-538-9091
www.micromuse.com

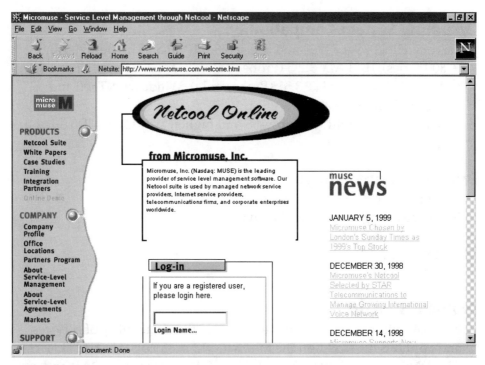

Figure 4.20 Micromuse, Incorporated, Web site.

Copyright Micromuse Inc. 1999.

Product Name:

Netcool Suite

Current Versions:

Netcool/OMNIbus (the core in-memory database application plus more than 50 Probes) 3.3

Netcool/Internet Service Monitors 1.1

Netcool/Mainframe Connection 1.0

Netcool/FireWall-1 1.0

Netcool/Service Views for Network Node Manager 1.0

Netcool/Reporter 1.1

Operating System Compatibility:

Servers: HP UX 9.0.7 (700 and 800 series), 10.10 and higher (700 and 800 series); IBM AIX 3.2.5 (Probes only), AIX 4.2; Solaris 1.1.1, 2.4, 2.5, 2.51; Windows NT 3.51 (Probes only), Windows NT 4.0 and higher, (Windows 2000)

Desktops: OSF/Motif, Windows95 and higher, Windows NT 3.5.1, 4.0, and higher

Browser Compatibility:

Internet Explorer 3.0 and above

Netscape Navigator 3.01 and above

Java Enabled?

Yes, 100 percent

Protocol Support:

Netcool/Internet Service Monitors ensure the availability of services and applications based on the following 12 protocols: HTTP, HTTP-S, FTP, DNS, NNTP, POP3, SMTP, RADIUS, Ping, IMAP4, LDAP, and a TCP Port Monitor.

Product Vis-à-Vis RMON:

The product collects management data from RMON1 and RMON2 and displays it in the Netcool EventList. Netcool has no competitive relationship with RMON. Netcool collects information from more than 50 management environments off the shelf, including:

- SNMP-based managers (SPECTRUM, OpenView, SunNet Manager, NetView, etc.)
- WAN and voice environments (StrataView, Newbridge, Nortel, Siemens, Timeplex, Ericsson, etc.)
- Internet service monitors (HTTP, FTP, etc. previously listed)
- Databases and management applications (Oracle, Sybase, Informix, Windows NT, BMC Patrol, etc.)

Suggested Applications and Important Information:

The Netcool suite of applications is used by managers and operators in network operating centers (NOCs) to ensure availability of network-based user services and business applications. The company's current target market is service providers—ISPs, telcos, carriers, cellular carriers, managed network service providers, and network outsourcers, as well as traditional corporate enterprises.

Out of the box, Netcool provides real-time Internet availability information on 12 Internet protocols and applications by regularly testing that each service is available for use. The program includes six new Monitors, including HTTP-S, IMAP4, RADIUS, LDAP, Ping, and a Port Monitor. These are packaged with the original six Monitors: DNS, FTP, HTTP, POP3, SMTP, and NNTP. Each Monitor adheres to the Internet Engineering Task Force (IETF) Request for Comment (RFC) for its associated protocol, and is based on an open, client-server architecture.

Major enhancements in the existing version include centralized configuration and viewing tools, support for multiple profiles, a new reporting mechanism, and increased flexibility for existing Monitors.

It allows operators to custom-design views of services, providing them with summaries of service availability or details of network-based events, enabling them to circumvent service outages. A key feature of the product is the ability to perform *time-domain* correlation of Internet services. Time-domain correlation is a menu-driven function that shows a summary of the availability of a given service—and all events underlying that service— since the last time that service was reported as good.

The predefined default intervals for which Netcool/ISMs begin collecting response time and availability data represent current best-business practices in the Internet industry. In addition, Netcool/ISMs can be dynamically configured using browsers such as Netscape Navigator or Microsoft Internet Explorer. Service-level management is the effective monitoring and management of multiple elements underlying the enterprise infrastructure—including network devices, computing systems, and applications—and the mapping of these elements to the business services they impact. Netcool's focus is on providing an efficient technology solution to the complex customer-to-service provider business paradigm. Its distributed architecture allows network operators to custom design real-time views of enterprisewide services. These views provide operators with summaries of service availability and details of network-based events, enabling them to circumvent service outages. A service might be an end-to-end application, a digital transmission service, a business unit, a virtual private network, or an Internet connection.

Netcool, which runs under Unix, Windows NT, or Java, is based on an open, client/server architecture. It features lightweight supersets of code called *Probes* that collect enterprisewide event messages in an object-based, high-speed, active database called the *ObjectServer*. The ObjectServer normalizes events into a common data format called the *EventList*. Operators use drag-and-drop filtering tools to manipulate ObjectServer data to create service views and reports on service-level availability. As networks grow, Probes and ObjectServers scale linearly, allowing service providers to expand their networks without hiring more personnel.

NetOps Corporation

Pleasantville, NY
Tel: 914-747-7600
Fax: 914-747-7627
www.netops.com

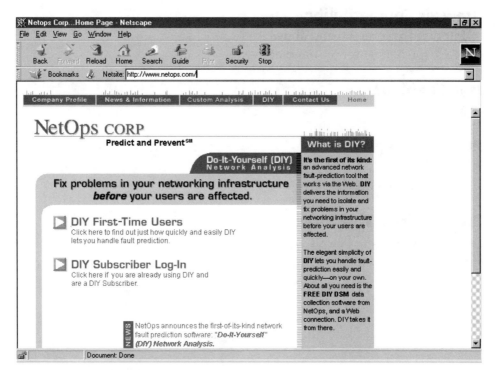

Figure 4.21 NetOps Corporation Web site.
Source: Courtesy of NetOps Corp.

Product Name:

Do-It-Yourself (DIY) Network Analysis

Current Version:

1.0.

Version 2.0 is expected out in the first quarter of 1999.

Operating System Compatibility:

Service will add device-specific templates for any device that the product does not already include.

Browser Compatibility:

Internet Explorer 3.0 and above

Netscape Navigator 3.01 and above

Java Enabled?

Yes

Protocol Support:

SNMP

Also monitors frame relay

Product Vis-à-Vis RMON:

DIY is not RMON based.

Suggested Applications and Important Information:

DIY's Distributed Status Monitor (DSM) allows a manager to check about 1000 status indicators per second across a typical network. The DSM software acts in the background with virtually no impact on bandwidth or CPU utilization. The software automatically models network devices, letting the manager target specific SNMP devices and adjust data collection intervals to local requirements.

Analysis reports are generated and displayed online, with a Problem Summary Report to outline problems detected by the analysis. Problems are reported in order of severity. The network manager then can drill down into each problem for a more detailed explanation. The best feature in this area is the recommendations that are included for addressing and correcting each problem.

Since this is a service, the billing is based on a pay-as-you-go basis. There is a flat-fee transaction charge with additions for the number of *billable devices* monitored in the network. A billable device is a monitored IP address with up to 64 ports or interfaces. The 65th, 129th, and so on begin a new billable service. The other factor is the total number of whole or partial weeks that the data spans. There is a $500 flat fee for any data upload, plus $20 per device for each week's worth of data. For example, to analyze a week's data with 6 IP addresses (1 with 64 interfaces, 2 with 65 ports, and 3 with 257 ports) would cost $900: $500 for the transaction fee, $20 for device 1, $40 each for devices 2 and 3, and $100 each for the 3 with 257 ports.

What do you get for the money? On a high-end router or switch, DIY models 800 to 1000 MIB objects and looks at 50 to 100 per target device at any given second. All of the data is correlated and analyzed for all of the devices on the network, not just one MIB object at a time. That ability to analyze and correlate data gives DIY the ability to focus on more complex problems, like routing convergence, and to offer cause and effect diagnosis.

DSM serves as midlevel managers capable of reporting events to any SNMP-capable enterprise manager. The system defines the thresholds that flag potential problems with the objects. It also allows on-demand analysis of problems or areas of concern defined by the network manager. The product will do availability analysis (measuring not only whether a box and its interfaces is up, but also the effects of routing instability—Border Gateway Protocol (BGP) and Open Shortest Path First (OSPF)—on each device. The product also does capacity planning as it relates to faults.

AT&T will offer DIY as part of the AT&T Solutions package. The company suggests weekly analysis of most networks to give time to spot and repair early-stage faults in the network.

NetScout Systems, Incorporated

Westford, MA
Tel: 978-614-4000
Fax: 978-614-4004
www.netscout.com

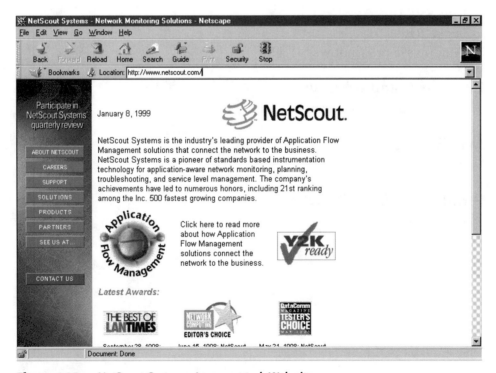

Figure 4.22a   NetScout Systems, Incorporated, Web site.

Product Name:
NetScout Manager Plus

Current Version:
5.2

Operating System Compatibility:
Sun OS 4.1.3
Solaris 2.5.1
HP UX 9.0.5
AIX 4.1
Unix SVR4
Digital Unix 3.0
Windows95 or Windows NT 4.0

Browser Compatibility:
Planned future enhancement

Java Enabled?
No

Product Vis-à-Vis RMON:
RMON/RMON2

Suggested Applications and Important Information:

NetScout Manager Plus, the console software at the heart of the NetScout Manager family, monitors, analyzes, and reports on data gathered from RMON probes throughout a company's network. The product uses a suite of 40 integrated applications to give information required for trouble-shooting, managing Service Level Agreements (SLAs), performance tuning and capacity planning, and enforcing network policies.

NetScout probes monitor LANs, switched LANs, WANs, and frame relay circuits. They track the use of any protocol or application running on the network. Using an integrated, multivendor approach, the product monitors fast Ethernet and VLAN segments. In addition, it is possible to track network usage over time, providing a host of baseline statistics for future capacity planning, billing, or long-term trend analysis.

NetScout Probes offer end-to-end monitoring needed to simplify net-work troubleshooting and capacity planning. Proactive, real-time monitor-ing of all network traffic attributes provides the diagnostic information required to pinpoint a problem before it affects network performance.

The probes support the full seven-layer traffic monitoring defined by the RMON2 standard, allowing technicians to track host, conversation, and application usage end to end, even across routers.

The product's architecture specifies real-time monitoring and diagnostic troubleshooting for the switched infrastructure, providing visibility into all switch ports, interswitch trunks, and server lines without burdening the switch. In this way, the NetScout Probes add value to switching devices from switch manufacturers such as Cisco, DEC, Newbridge Networks, Fore Systems, 3Com, Cabletron, Bay Networks, and the like.

The company also offers AppScout, an application flow monitor. It is browser based and provides an easy entree into following the status of the network. The manufacturer emphasizes that AppScout is not a replace-ment for NetScout Manager Plus since it does not support the extensive examination of traffic parameters, conversation lists, frame capture, and protocol analysis that the full package does. However, it is a good supple-ment for network operations. It gives a complete status and health view for those outside network operations who need to understand the perfor-mance of networked applications.

NetScout Systems, Incorporated

Westford, MA
Tel: 978-614-4000
Fax: 978-614-4004
www.netscout.com

Figure 4.22b   NetScout Systems, Incorporated, Web site.

Product Name:

AppScout application flow monitor

Current Version:

1.0

Operating System Compatibility:

Solaris 2.5.1 and higher
Windows NT 4.0

Browser Compatibility:

Browser independent; reliance is on JDK 1.1.4 or AWT 1.1.4

Java Enabled?

Yes

Protocol Support:

All TCP-based applications, NFS and RPC

Product Vis-à-Vis RMON:

AppScout measures actual conversations of networked applications. It
does not emulate or simulate application traffic. AppScout leverages
data acquired from ART MIB-enabled RMON probes.

Suggested Applications and Important Information:

AppScout is network monitoring software that provides real-time, Web-based access to information on application performance over an enterprise network. AppScout tracks and presents a comprehensive view of real application traffic flows and identifies the impact that an application has on the network, as well as the network's impact on the application. Specifically, AppScout provides the following views and information:

- Network visibility by application, location, client, and server
- Multidimensional views of network health, including link quality and network flight time displays and application response times
- Historical references
- Threshold alerts for response-time performance

AppScout provides a shared perspective, from which network and application managers can understand the extent to which applications are leveraging and impacting the power of the network. AppScout performs the following functions:

- Measures application and server response times
- Correlates information from multiple sources
- Delivers intuitive, real-time, Web-based reports
- Identifies the source of performance problems
- Leverages existing network instrumentation
- Extends to all topologies for the broadest media coverage

NetScout Systems, Incorporated

Westford, MA
Tel: 978-614-4000
Fax: 978-614-4004
www.netscout.com

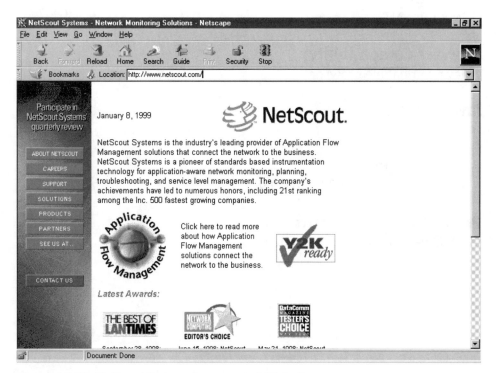

Figure 4.22c   NetScout Systems, Incorporated, Web site.

Product Name:
WebCast

Current Version:
1.1

Operating System Compatibility:
Sun OS 4.1x
Solaris 2.3
HP UX 9.9
AIX 3.2.4
Windows NT

Browser Compatibility:
Java-compatible browser

Java Enabled?
Yes

Protocol Support:
Everything supported by RMON

Product Vis-à-Vis RMON:
RMON- and RMON2-dependent

Suggested Applications and Important Information:

Web-based reporting for RMON/RMON2 data

Network Associates, Incorporated

Santa Clara, CA
Tel: 408-988-3832
www.nai.com

Figure 4.23   Network Associates, Incorporated, Web site.

Product Name:

Sniffer Service Desk

Current Version:

1.0
Version 2.0 is due out first quarter of 1999.

Operating System Compatibility:

Server: NT 4.0 server
Client: Web-based console to view reports

Browser Compatibility:

Internet Explorer 4.0
Netscape Navigator 4.0

Java Enabled?

No

Protocol Support:

Standard RMON2 protocol support

Systems Compatibility:

HP OpenView

Product Vis-à-Vis RMON:

Utilizes RMON1 and RMON2 data for traffic monitoring and SNMP
data for device monitoring. RouterPM also provides device and
network analysis based on gathered RMON data.

Suggested Applications and Important Information:

The Sniffer Service Desk offers network performance monitoring with high-level reporting, exception reporting, and alerts. The product provides customizable Web-based reporting that allows IT managers to manage service levels, control costs, and proactively manage network health and availability. The manufacturer says the product is the first Windows NT–based enterprise reporting and analysis tool to enable IT personnel to proactively monitor and address network health through analysis of real-time and historical data, by integrating with Network Associates' leading Sniffer Expert Analysis technology and RMON2 monitoring capabilities.

Novadigm, Incorporated

Mahwah, NJ
Emeryville, CA
Tel: 800-626-NOVA; 201-512-1000
Fax: 201-512-1001
www.novadigm.com

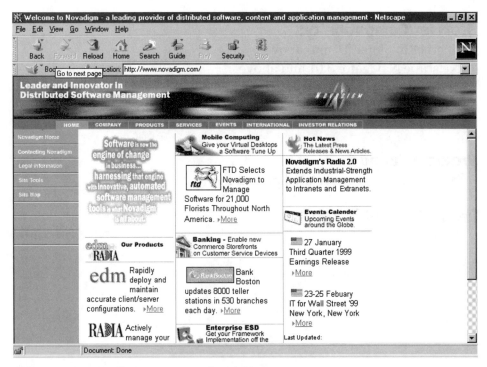

Figure 4.24   Novadigm, Incorporated, Web site.

Product Name:
Radia Software Manager

Current Version:
2.0

Operating System Compatibility:
UNIX
Solaris
HP UX
Windows NT 4.0

Browser Compatibility:
Internet Explorer 3.0 and above
Netscape Navigator 3.01 and above

Java Enabled?
Yes

Protocol Support:
Works with any Java-related protocol.

Product Vis-à-Vis RMON:
N/A

Suggested Applications and Important Information:

The Radia Software Manager's Radia 2.0 enables companies to manage desktops inside and outside their enterprise by automatically adapting user software and content to changes from all directions. The result is highly reliable, personalized software and content for every user needing secure access to enterprise applications. The suite of electronic software management products combines the benefits of highly reliable, large-scale software distribution and management across the Internet with the advantages of personalized management of software for each end-user desktop. Radia 2.0 includes the initial release of Radia Application Manager and the general release of Radia Software Manager.

Radia Application Manager provides a highly robust software management environment, enabling companies to share applications and information with partners, suppliers, customers, and other extranet users. It automatically adapts software to meet individual user needs and policy requirements while ensuring better than 99 percent availability.

Radia Software Manager gives end users—such as knowledge workers, mobile users, and remote office personnel—the ability to select and personally configure software products and content from Internet-based software catalogs prepared by internal or external providers. Once on the users' desktops, these applications and content are automatically updated by Radia Software Manager as necessary with no user intervention required. Driving the 2.0 product is Novadigm's patented *Desired State Engine* based on the company's Enterprise Desktop Manager (EDM) 4.0. Novadigm offers its integrated set of software management solutions based on a single technology platform. Its Radia products and Enterprise Desktop Manager (EDM) use adaptive configuration technology to deliver high-level automation of software distribution and management, resulting in near-perfect application reliability without local oversight. No matter what users do to "break" their individual desktops, such as deleting files, installing conflicting software, or changing their desktop configurations, these products automatically identify the problems or incompatibilities and then adjust the desktop "just in time" for sustained productivity.

The software dynamically discovers the status of each user's system (its *actual state* of current software, configurations, and content) and compares this in real time with a model of its *desired state* (the software and content that the system should have). If there is a difference between the two, the product will automatically determine the precise changes that are required and, using *fractional differencing* technology, send only those changes to fix the user's desktop. For each Radia product the initial license fee for PC clients is $75 per user. The manufacturer says additional Radia products will be announced in the near future to meet the emerging software management needs of distributed enterprises and specialized markets, including revisable-content publishers, Internet service providers, and independent software vendors.

Novazen, Incorporated

Boulder, CO
Tel: 303-583-3100
www.novazen.com

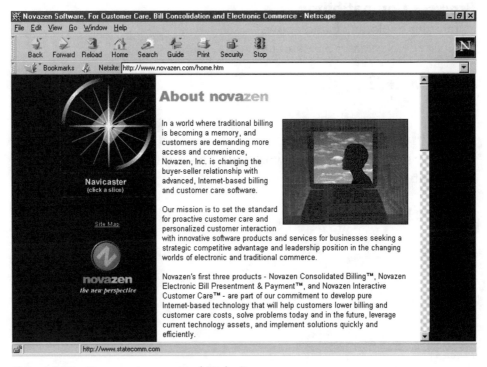

Figure 4.25   Novazen, Incorporated, Web site.

Product Name:
Interactive Customer Care

Current Version:
1.0

Operating System Compatibility:
Sun Solaris
HP UX
Windows NT

Browser Compatibility:
Internet Explorer 3.0 and above
Netscape Navigator 3.01 and above

Java Enabled?
Yes

Protocol Support:
Vendor states that products work with most billing and statement generation systems.

Product Vis-à-Vis RMON:
N/A

Suggested Applications and Important Information:

This is quite a specific Web-based application. The current suite of Novazen, Inc. products includes Interactive Customer Care, Electronic Bill Presentment and Payment, and Consolidated Billing. The Internet-based customer care products are aimed specifically at letting companies extend Web-based solutions to their customer base, including self-service bill-back checks and billing options. All company-to-customer interactions and activities can be performed via the Internet or over the phone. Both the customer and the customer service representative (CSR) see the same thing on their screens at the same time.

The company's Consolidated Billing and Electronic Bill Presentment modules let carriers consolidate bills from across a range of products and services and present a single, customized bill over the Internet. The Consolidated Billing product will accept billing data from several sources, including relational or object databases, legacy systems, flat files, or mag tape. It then puts them into a single statement. The carrier then massages the bill presentment process (including bill formatting and design, automatic scheduling, and delivery of electronic bills) and sends the bill to the customer. The Interactive Customer Care product gives all the capacity needed to set up an online customer care center. It is based on object-oriented technology and integrates traditional call center functions with a Web-based customer care system, letting the end user access and self-manage accounts over the Internet. There is a default icon that allows the customer to initiate a session with a live CSR via an Internet chat session, Internet telephony, e-mail, or POTS call.

Phasecom, Incorporated

Cupertino, CA
Tel: 408-777-7784
Fax: 408-777-7787
www.speed-demon.com

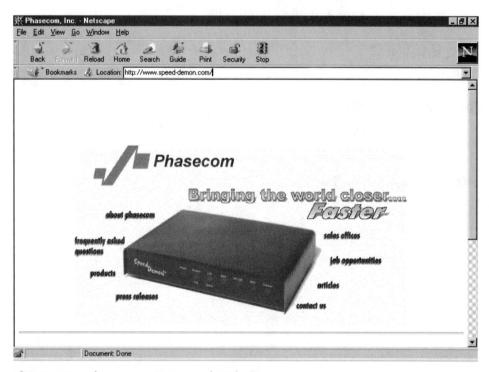

Figure 4.26   Phasecom, Incorporated, Web site.

Product Name:
CyberManage for SpeedDemon

Current Version:
1.0

Operating System Compatibility:
Works with Phasecom's SpeedDemon cable modems.

Browser Compatibility:
Internet Explorer 3.0 and above
Netscape Navigator 3.01 and above

Java Enabled?
Yes

Systems Compatibility:
In this configuration, works only with the SpeedDemon cable modem system.

Product Vis-à-Vis RMON:
Can accommodate RMON MIBs

Suggested Applications and Important Information:

Equipped with CyberManage from Wipro (see Wipro listing), Phasecom's SpeedDemon cable modems and cable modem termination systems (CMTS) can be remotely configured or managed from anywhere across the Internet. This will allow cable operators deploying cable modem systems to remotely monitor modems and CMTSs, in real time, from any PC through any standard Web browser.

In addition to remote management, cable operators can now track usage patterns, understand potential faults and alarms, and service these faults and alarms all in real time from a simple browser interface. Another key advantage of integrating the CyberManage platform with the SpeedDemon cable modem system is universal access to any network status information by various groups within the cable operator's organization. The tech support group can access information of any device in the network, the accounting group can get usage statistics on any individual cable modem customer for billing purposes, and the customer service organization can monitor traffic to and from any device to assure performance requirements—from a standard browser interface.

Pinnacle Software Corporation

Pittsford, NY
Tel: 716-381-2750
www.pinnsoft.com

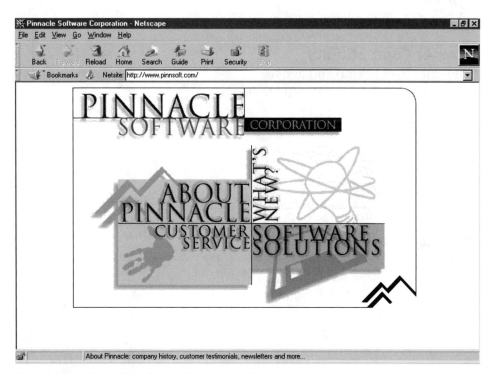

Figure 4.27   Pinnacle Software Corporation Web site.

Product Name:

Axis Web

Current Version:

1.0

Operating System Compatibility:

Windows NT
Sun Solaris
IBM AIX
HP UX
Variety of UNIX platforms

Browser Compatibility:

Internet Explorer 3.0 and above
Netscape Navigator 3.01 and above

Java Enabled?

Yes

Protocol Support:

Works with Axis Communication Systems

Product Vis-à-Vis RMON:

No

Suggested Applications and Important Information:

Axis Communications System allows systems administrators to quickly and easily manage long-distance resale, toll-fraud detection, and trouble tickets. Axis is a hardware-independent client/server system. It combines the power of the Oracle SQL database with a graphical user interface (GUI). Its Web functionality also enhances customer service and reduces or eliminates traditional hard-copy telecom reporting.

The foundation of the system's structure couples industry-standard relational database management with the most current client/server network technology. The Axis Telephone Manager provides detailed customer service windows; supports multiple carriers, online billing, and customer service inquiry; applies rate discounts by group; generates and prints bills; and tracks subscriber payments through accounts receivable. The Facilities Manager performs inventory, cable, work-order, and trouble-ticket management and reporting. Included are functions such as creating unlimited work-order and trouble-ticket types, tracking cable data to the component level, monitoring inventory in multiple warehouses, and generating multiple user-defined reports.

Axis Web is divided into three distinct areas, making it easy for subscribers to locate areas of interest. Axis Web Customer Service lets subscribers view accrued charges to date, view and print monthly statements (current and historical), and perform directory searches. Such customer service via the Web eliminates the need for internal staff to print, stuff, and sort statements, and it generally reduces the number of account query calls. The Axis Web Facilities Management program allows technicians to receive, review, and update work orders and trouble tickets. The Axis Web Systems Administration lets administrators monitor telemanagement functions from virtually anywhere, at any time. Administrators have the power to monitor users, provide basic database, and define Web security administration functions.

Sterling Software, Incorporated

Reston, VA
Tel: 800-247-5163; 703-264-8000
Fax: 703-476-0328
www.solve.sterling.com

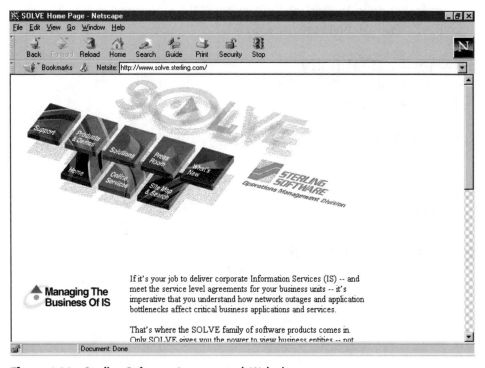

Figure 4.28   Sterling Software, Incorporated, Web site.

Product Name:

SOLVE:Netmaster for TCP/IP

Current Version:

Version 4.0 released October 31, 1998

Operating System Compatibility:

IBM's TCP/IP for MVS v3.1 or later

Interlink's TCPaccess 3.1 or later

Cisco's IOS for S/390 Release 1.0 or 2.0

For comprehensive network management, the product also can run in conjunction with Sterling Software's SOLVE:Netmaster for SNA or IBM's TME 10 NetView for OS/390.

Browser Compatibility:

Internet Explorer 3.0 and above

Netscape Navigator 3.01 and above

Java Enabled?

Yes, for Java scripts only

Protocol Support:

TCP/IP

Product Vis-à-Vis RMON:

This product does not support RMON.

Suggested Applications and Important Information:

SOLVE:Netmaster is primarily for mainframe-based operations that require a remote network management tool. It provides real-time access to network information via any Java-enabled Web browser.

SOLVE:Netmaster for TCP/IP combines extended performance management with comprehensive and easy-to-use TCP/IP management. The new performance option expands the product's existing performance feature to include out-of-the-box corporate intranet trending and capacity planning of both the physical network devices and logical network applications that support mission-critical enterprise business. Performance management enhancements are targeted at the operational requirements of managing mixed SNA and TCP/IP networks from OS/390.

SOLVE:Netmaster for TCP/IP offers management of the network infrastructure that enables intranet access to mainframe data by providing consolidated management of both TCP/IP and SNA environments. This allows visibility of end-user sessions all the way to an OS/390 application, and enables OS/390 application access to be conducted over the corporate intranet with levels of reliability and availability that are the hallmark of traditional mainframe systems and SNA networks.

Key new performance functionality in the product's next release will include the following:

- A new Graphical Performance Manager that will provide out-of-the-box reporting features to improve network manageability and reliability. Graphical reports will provide session traffic analysis, historical capacity planning, trend analysis, and network performance analysis.

- A Real-Time Performance Monitor that accumulates performance data and displays recent history of network utilization and performance. This will help improve network and application reliability by identifying potential device problems that may be affecting the use of OS/390-based applications.

■ A new Intelligent Performance Manager to proactively monitor network performance via rules-based auditing and alerting of network metrics, such as IP response time and network volume. These metrics are then compared against predefined utilization thresholds to generate alerts and invoke automated actions.

With this enhanced support, Sterling Software continues to ensure that customers moving to a mixed SNA and TCP/IP environment can address the growing need to share information between mainframe and distributed environments. SOLVE:Netmaster for TCP/IP is the only enterprise-based product to provide manageability of the Cisco TN3270 Server, in addition to proactive performance management of routers, and support for Cisco's IOS for S/390.

N-Vision does require a Java-enabled Web browser on Windows NT, Windows95 or on a Unix-based platform.

A look at the rough pricing for the product puts SOLVE:Netmaster for TCP/IP's starting price at $30,000 based on CPU model group. The fees vary depending on the number of concurrent users. An unlimited site license also is available.

Telco Research Corporation

Nashville, TN
Tel: 800-488-3526; 615-872-9000
Fax: 615-231-6144
www.telcoresearch.com

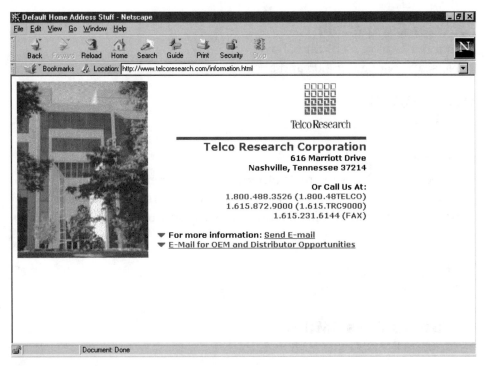

Figure 4.29   Telco Research Corporation Web site.

Source: Telco Research Corporation

Product Name:

TRU Enterprise Network Accountant (TRU ENA)

Current Version:

1.0

Operating System Compatibility:

Web server hardware: Windows NT
Web server software: Microsoft IIS 4.0, Netscape Enterprise 3.0, or
    FastTrack servers
Client software: Java-enabled browser

Browser Compatibility:

Internet Explorer 4.01 and above
Netscape Navigator 4.05 and above

Java Enabled?

Java-based

Systems Compatibility:

Works with Telco Research's other telemanagement and network
accounting product lines. The information gathered is rolled into those
products. Standard APIs allow users to import from virtually any data
source.

Protocol Support:

Supports SNMP and the RMON suites

Product Vis-à-Vis RMON:

Supports RMON1 and RMON2

Suggested Applications and Important Information:

The TRU Enterprise Network Accountant provides managers browser access to a consolidated database of enterprisewide data and voice-call detail records. This is a Java-based reporting tool that provides a consolidated view of companywide voice (telephone, fax) and data (e-mail, Web) usage patterns and associated costs. Using a browser, department managers and upper management have easy access to summary and detailed phone and Internet usage data. They can view summary usage and accounting data for any or all departments and drill down to view CDR reports in HTML format.

The uniqueness of this application is the presentation and consolidation of accounting data from disparate device management applications through a corporate intranet. Telecom or IT managers can gather telephone and Internet call record information from network collection devices such as PBXs, Centrex systems, routers, firewalls, remote access servers, and network access servers.

This data is rolled up into management applications including other Telco Research product lines. Costed call detail records generated by these applications are stored in a database that can be accessed by managers using the TRU ENA product. Department managers can be restricted to viewing only information related to their respective departments.

TRU ENA uses Java technology to ensure maximum client/platform compatibility. In keeping with an open network accounting strategy, data is not only collected from a wide variety of network devices, the data can also be exported to other programs, like Excel, where it can be further manipulated. This product uses industry-standard Crystal Reports to generate four report classes: (1) Subscriber, (2) Organization, (3) Account Code, and (4) Charge Type.

The TRU ENA price is $7500 to $25,000 depending on network configuration.

Collecting, consolidating, and reporting IT service-related data is escalating in priority for many IT managers. Faced with increasing challenges to the quality of service they provide and the associated costs, IT managers must educate and inform their users on the effective use of these services. TRU ENA provides the foundation and framework to consolidate and publish IT service-related data over a secured intranet. It provides department managers immediate access to IT service-related data for enforcing policies, reviewing budgets, and planning future expenses. Consisting of many standard end-user features, TRU ENA also provides compatibility with common desktop utilities for extended or advanced analysis.

Once installed, TRU ENA provides virtually an administration-free environment for publishing IT related service information.

Tivoli Systems, Incorporated

Austin, TX
Tel: 800-2-TIVOLI; 512-794-9070
Fax: 512-794-0623
www.tivoli.com

Figure 4.30   Tivoli Systems, Incorporated, Web site.

Product Name:

Tivoli Distributed Monitoring and Enterprise Management Suite

Current Version:

Tivoli Enterprise 3.6

Operating System Compatibility:

Sun Solaris, SunOS
HP UX
IBM AIX, OS/2, AS/400
Microsoft Windows NT
Windows95
Novell NetWare
Multiple Unix platforms

Browser Compatibility:

Internet Explorer 4.0 and above
Netscape Navigator 4.02 and above

Java Enabled?

Yes

Protocol Support:

TCP/IP
IPX

Systems Compatibility:

Sun Solaris, SunOS
HP UX
IBM AIX
Microsoft Windows NT
Multiple Unix platforms

Product Vis-à-Vis RMON:

RMON-compatible modules are available.

Suggested Applications and Important Information:

Tivoli Distributed Monitoring provides an easy, consistent way to monitor and manage key distributed resources through a centralized management interface. The complete monitoring solution includes Tivoli Distributed Monitoring; Tivoli Decision Support for Reporting; and Tivoli Enterprise Console for Event Consolidation, Escalation, Automation, and Root-Cause Analysis. A newly released product, Tivoli Manager for Network Connectivity, provides program-free, maintenance-free, automated root-cause determination of network outages.

The large collection of prepackaged monitors enables you to configure monitoring parameters for groups of systems. You also can add custom monitors that do not require complex integration. Monitoring parameters can be set and updated for an entire group and applied to all the distributed resources in a single action. Changes to hundreds of related remote systems take place in minutes—ensuring consistency across all target systems.

Its mergers with companies like IBM, Unison, and Software Artistry enable Tivoli to extend and fortify its set of products and services, ushering in a new era in open computing. Tivoli now delivers the first true, end-to-end management solution, which includes a single, standard, unified method for managing everything from desktop PCs and laptops to data center mainframes.

The product fully supports the Application Management Specification, an industry standard that enables you to define a standard data structure and format to make applications management-ready. Tivoli Distributed Monitoring also includes Application Response Measurement technology, allowing you to measure application transaction response time across multiple distributed components and take automated, corrective actions when application response times fail to meet required service levels.

Tivoli Distributed Monitoring allows you to specify critical resource thresholds that automatically trigger customized corrective and preventive actions upon detection of conditions that threaten applications availability or service levels in your environment. The product includes Inspector—a powerful graphical trend-analysis tool accessible via a Web browser. Inspector allows you to remotely access and troubleshoot distributed systems and provides a graphical representation of multiple metrics on one or more distributed systems. This visual representation of real-time information quickly leads you to a clear understanding of the problem situation, so you can take the necessary corrective actions.

There are additional plug-in modules available for DB2, Sybase, Oracle, Informix, MS SQL Server, Microsoft Exchange, R/3, Domino, MQSeries, MCIS, and SuiteSpot.

Wipro Corporation

Santa Clara, CA
Tel: 408-557-4409
Fax: 408-615-7174
www.wipro.com

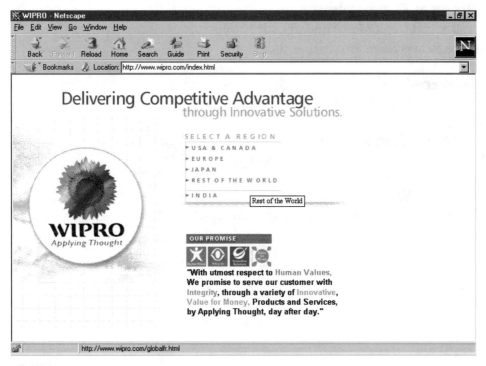

Figure 4.31   Wipro Corporation Web site.

Product Name:
CyberManage

Current Version:
3.0

Operating System Compatibility:
Windows NT 4.0 (or higher)
Windows95
Solaris 2.6 with JDK 1.1 support

Browser Compatibility:
Internet Explorer 3.0 and above
Netscape Navigator 3.01 and above

Java Enabled?
Yes. Works with any Java-enabled browser.

Systems Compatibility:
Works with any Java-compatible system

Product Vis-à-Vis RMON:
Includes provisions for accommodating RMON MIBs

Suggested Applications and Important Information:

The CyberManage Platform is a Java-based network management platform with a built-in HTTP server. Once the platform is installed, all a manager needs to do is connect a browser to the CyberManage URL. The CyberManage Platform interprets and translates HTTP requests from the browser to SNMP requests over the network and vice versa. It also has a set of Java applets that perform network management functions such as topology discovery, fault handling, and event management.

This product allows SNMP-based networks and networked devices—routers, hubs, systems, modems, UPSs, and printers—to be managed within an intranet or across the Internet. It runs on any machine supporting the Java Runtime Environment (JRE) and provides a rich set of features, all of which can be accessed from your favorite Web browser. The package ships with generic device management applications for MIB II-compliant devices. It includes support for network management features such as topology discovery, event management, graphing, and sending alerts via a pager, e-mail, or a message to the designated fax machine.

The product offers full database integration, with the ability to export management information gathered by CyberManage to any JBDC-compliant database. It is fully standards compliant: RFC 1155 (SNMP), RFC 1630 (URI Syntax), RFC 1738 (URL), RFC 1808 (Relative URL), RFC 1866 (HTML), and RFC 1945 (HTTP Version 1.1).

Providing device and network management solutions using Internet technologies is one of Wipro's key initiatives. A Java applet enables real-time graphical display of device parameters. Support is available for bar graphs, line graphs, and gauges.

Not only does the product support many computer languages, it also offers multilingual human language support. This allows management of the network in English, Japanese, or French—perfect for follow-the-sun applications.

The company's Technology Solutions Division is one of the 14 organizations globally that have been assessed at Software Engineering Institute—Capability Maturity Model (SEI-CMM) Level 4.

Xedia Corporation

Littleton, MA
Tel: 508-952-6000; 800-98-XEDIA
www.xedia.com

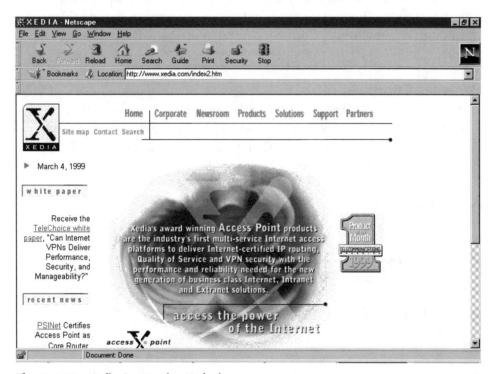

Figure 4.32   Xedia Corporation Web site.

Product Name:

Access Point

Current Version:

Release 1.5.

Release 2.0 is slated to be available first quarter of 1999.

Operating System Compatibility:

Access Point is a bandwidth management platform with routing capabilities that is based on the MIPS R5000 processor, running PSOS. There are multiple ways of configuring the platform and monitoring traffic classes. The two most common ways of accomplishing this is through Access Point's Command Line Interface (CLI) or through its integrated Web-based management system.

Browser Compatibility:

The Web-based interface is accessible through any browser that supports frames and Java. The product has been extensively tested with Netscape Communicator (Solaris 2.5.1, Windows 4.0) and Microsoft Internet Explorer (Windows 4.0).

Java Enabled?

Yes

Protocol Support:

See comments under Browser Compatibility

Product Vis-à-Vis RMON:

N/A

Suggested Applications and Important Information:

The product's Web-based interface may be used for configuration of any Access Point parameters. It is best used for ease of use in configuring traffic classes and subsequently for monitoring network traffic being passed through each of the classes. Access Point keeps very detailed statistics on a per-traffic-class basis, which may be viewed through the Web-based interface. In addition, in Release 1.5, Xedia is introducing a new *Traffic Equalizer* capability that shows the instantaneous utilization levels for a set of traffic classes, as well as the aggregate level for all of the individual traffic classes displayed.

The Web-based interface and the Traffic Equalizer are included in the price of an Access Point system. Access Point has a list price ranging from $4995 to $19,995, depending upon configuration and performance level. Release 2.0, slated to be available in the first quarter of 1999, will introduce Virtual Private Networking (VPN) functionality to the Access Point platform. Xedia's VPN support will include IPSec for dial-in and site-to-site tunneling and authentication, software and high-speed encryption (DES and Triple-DES) support, and RADIUS support for user authentication and configuration. This release will also include support for IP Network Address Translation (NAT).

How Real Users Take
Advantage of Web-Based
Management

Visits to vendors' operations and abstract reviews of product capabilities on paper are nice, but they lack the stamp of real-world application. Seeing is believing, and much of the reason for visiting any site in the world of Web-based management is to see how systems work in the user's own operation. Fortunately, this is one area where the technology has advanced beyond the realm of vaporware and into practical applications of the technology in major institutional settings.

It is in the network management center where the proverbial rubber meets the proverbial road. A host of enterprises—including gas and electric utilities, the Trump property management consortium, a Web development company, a racing consortium, and the *New York Times*—are making successful use of Web-based management in their networks. In every case, the systems administrators have a bit of "I don't know how we did it until we went Web-based" in their voices as they describe their systems.

This chapter, then, is the reality check for all of the other information in this book. The proof of the pudding is in the eating—and the firms in this chapter are lapping up the Web-based management concept and find that it more than suits their needs.

These companies were open to sharing their goals, fears, and the specific products and strategies they used to make their Web-based management systems operate according to their individual needs. In each case, the size, scope, and focus of the program is a bit different. However, in every case the solution came down to meeting a management challenge with a Web-based management solution. When your operation has narrowed down its buying decision to two or three firms, it would be a good idea to contact several users of their products and interview them on what they think of the Web-based management products they are using. Be sure to ask what hurdles they had to overcome in such areas as installation, training, compatibility, and service calls. Ask about changes they hope to see in future versions of the product.

Meantime, here is a summary of how a select group of innovators implemented Web-based management and the benefits they reaped.

Two Utilities Use the Web

Two utilities recently chose the same product to accomplish their network management goals. Both were dealing with a complex lot of protocols, including TCP/IP and NetWare on a wide range of computing hardware. Although it is interesting that they chose the same product to help them reach their goals, both demonstrate the need for a good, overall umbrella approach to network management.

The Jacksonville Electric Authority (JEA) is Florida's largest municipally owned electric power and water utility. JEA owns, operates, and manages the electric system established by the City of Jacksonville in 1895. Compared to other municipally owned electric utilities, JEA is Florida's largest and the eighth largest in the United States, currently serving more than 340,000 customers in Jacksonville and parts of three adjacent counties.

After a seven-month product evaluation and planning process, JEA decided to standardize on Computer Associates' Unicenter TNG to manage and ensure the availability of critical systems across its heterogeneous computing environment.

"We needed to monitor and manage everything seamlessly," says the systems project leader. The need for an integrated, end-to-end IT management solution arose from JEA's recent migration to a distributed, open-architecture computing infrastructure. JEA has implemented a modern client/server environment to replace mission-critical legacy applications residing on its IBM and Unisys mainframes. In a little more than two years, the utility's IT environment has grown from 2 mainframes, 40 Novell servers, and 950 PCs to more than 1500 desktops, 60 Windows NT servers,

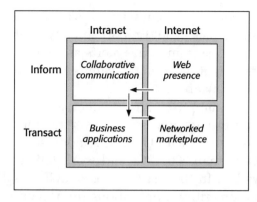

Figure 5.1   Framework for business users.
Source: Sun Microsystems

30 Novell servers, and 4 HP 9000 K-class systems. JEA's end users are interconnected via regional ATM, TCP/IP, and Novell NetWare IPX networks. A typical framework for business users is demonstrated in Figure 5.1.

JEA had to find a complete IT management solution that would help improve its services for more than 340,000 electric power customers, 170,000 water services customers, and 120,000 sewer services customers while maintaining a strict employment cap. The move has enabled it to keep IT staff levels relatively stable throughout the entire IT modernization process. It has provided a means to work smarter with the people JEA has, and to do a better job in the process.

Baltimore Gas & Electric Co. (BGE)—Maryland's largest power supplier—also adopted Computer Associates' Unicenter TNG as the solution of choice for managing its highly diverse and complex heterogeneous computing environment. The director sees Unicenter TNG as the mainstay for ensuring greater systems availability at BGE. BGE's business today means doing business continuously. Its customers depend on it to process information flawlessly, and on time. BGE has high expectations to provide optimal stability for its entire IT enterprise, allowing it to provide the highest quality service levels possible.

Founded in 1816, BGE is the nation's first gas utility and one of its earliest electric utilities, with a tradition of superior, low-cost service and reliability. With assets of more than $8 billion and nearly 8000 employees, BGE serves more than 1 million business and residential electric customers and 557,000 gas customers in an economically diverse, 2300-square-mile area encompassing Baltimore City and all or part of 10 Central Maryland counties. BGE delivers electricity and natural gas to more than 2.6 million residents throughout a 2300-square-mile area. Its diverse systems and networks must be up and running continuously, 365 days a year.

Until recently, its senior management felt as though they were in a reactive mode. The only way they knew about a problem with a disk drive, a server, or some other device was when a user would report some type of difficulty with the system. Now, the Web system issues alerts as soon as there is any indication that something might be wrong, meaning they can fix a potential problem before any user is aware of it.

BGE's IT network connects 5 main campuses and 30 remote sites, encompassing 200 local area networks in all. Its processing power includes a mix of IBM/MVS mainframe systems, along with HP-UX, Windows NT, and Novell NetWare servers, and more than 5000 PCs and workstations running Windows 3.1 and Windows NT. In the last five years, BGE has aggressively moved many of its mission-critical applications from mainframe to distributed client/server systems. As these applications have proliferated in number, diversity, and complexity, the utility's need for a unified and integrated approach to monitoring operations around the clock has become acute.

BGE realized that relying on a hodgepodge of independent management tools and scattered information on its networks, applications, databases, and connected devices was no longer acceptable. BGE needed a solution that provided comprehensive, end-to-end management of all IT resources. With Web-based management, the director and staff will be able to proactively monitor BGE's multiple LANs, which are spread across the state. They wanted to be able to set critical usage thresholds and know when those thresholds were being approached so they could address potential problems immediately, and prevent outages.

Senior management and staff believe that Web management is providing them with the necessary tools to gather business-critical information on a consistent basis and that its broad capabilities will benefit virtually every area of their business, from technical support to finance and executive management.

The same concept played big at JEA because it needed a solution that was extensible across a wide variety of platforms and operating systems. JEA liked the product's superior workload management, scheduling, and event-monitoring capabilities. It turns out that JEA relies heavily on the product's event management console to monitor and respond proactively to system events and alarms.

LAN management capabilities were another major factor in JEA's decision. Its IT staff has configured Unicenter TNG to generate pager calls and e-mails to support personnel if events occur that require intervention.

In addition to its technical management capabilities, JEA's IT group appreciates the product's ease of use, which enables management and other nontechnical staff to leverage the product's benefits. It has configured the software to show the status of key applications, as well as their related network and system resources, to assist business managers throughout the company.

The group has written a special software agent to monitor the health of its real-time data historian. The Plant Information (PI) product from OSI Software that JEA had been using did not have the enterprise management integration capabilities required, and OSI was not planning to address the issue until an unspecified future release. Using the Unicenter TNG Agent Factory Software Development Kit (SDK), the group wrote an agent that allows it to monitor and manage the health of the system. The agent allows JEA to fully manage the PI system without dedicating a full-time human administrator.

JEA's software agents will monitor power plant processes and commercial customer power meters. These solutions will help reduce maintenance costs by immediately identifying process upsets and service interruptions, and notifying field crews so the problems can be repaired promptly and efficiently.

JEA executives believe that by providing such capabilities they recap the highest returns on their technology investment.

Web Developer Discusses Advantages

You are sick. The last thing you want to do is take the 30-minute drive down to the office, but if your network is down, business stops. In the past, you would be forced to go into the office in order to overlook operations, but that day has passed. Using the Web, today you can just grab your laptop, and a connection to the net, and access your company's network and servers from your warm, comfy bed.

The network administrator for ImageNation, Inc., a development company based in Cleveland, Ohio, specializing in multitier, client/server Web development, knows the importance of Web-based management applications from both the user's and developer's perspective.

Running a Microsoft NT Server network, with Microsoft Internet Information Server, Microsoft Exchange Server, and Microsoft's SQL server, ImageNation can control the user settings, webs created, e-mail accounts, and more over a browser. NT comes with a Web-based management application that allows the permitted user to view users, running applications, event logs, system performance, and more. The network administrator believes it's extremely useful to be able to take the pulse of the network from anywhere in the world. The administrator can control accounts, create, modify, and delete users, close applications, and even shut down the server remotely.

Being a Web development company, ImageNation created its own secure Web site allowing easy access to all of the management applications they need. The site includes access to prepackaged Web-based management tools like NT's Web administration tool, as well as its own custom management tools. Security is of obvious import to such a system. ImageNation utilizes NT challenge-response, as well as the Secure Socket Layer, in order to protect against hacks and unauthorized usage.

Managing contacts, billing and hours, employee forms, sales publications, system accounts, projects, domain names, and e-mail are essential for ImageNation's operation. Using any browser, an ImageNation administrator can access these tools worldwide.

Browser Basics

The Web has grown so quickly that standards are still trying to catch up with the latest browser technology. The two main competitors in the browser wars are Microsoft, with Internet Explorer, and Netscape, with Navigator. Basic Web pages and server-side Web applications can be utilized on any browser, but when you want to have the latest user-interaction ability, a decision on which browser to support must be made.

Client-Side Web Programming

If you like dragging and dropping, immediate reaction of Web forms and other Web components without the download wait between pages, the latest browsers can give it to you, but only if the programmer codes these elements for the latest browsers.

If you program with the latest version of either browser in mind, the capabilities are virtually limitless. Browser technology has come a long way, and is continuously being enhanced. If you want universal Web application browser support, you must consider server-side programming.

Server-Side Web Programming

By having the server process information prior to delivering it to the client's Web browser, virtually any browser can utilize applications such as Web-based management systems. The browser then gains the power of the server, and its information processing capabilities.

Distributed Web Programming

The Web, by its nature, is distributed in its processing of components. Any Web browser can take text and format it, and the Web server utilizes information stored on it, or another machine, to deliver it to the client.

The Web, using a combination of server-side and client-side programming, can become a very powerful tool. You can access multiple computers, gather appropriate information, deliver that processed information to the client's machine, and allow the client to manipulate objects, rotate graphs, and change business scenarios—that is some of the power existing in multitier client/server development and distributed processing.

ImageNation has a special Web-based management site under development, still awaiting the implementation of some custom tools. The site allows the user to simulate management of an NT server on the Web. A closer look can be found at www.imagenationinc.com/webmgmt.

The good news at ImageNation is that the program works on the human and technology sides. The big news at the *New York Times* is that Web-based management works on both the technology and management sides.

The *New York Times* Addresses Security

Every morning the director of network services for the *New York Times* wakes up, puts on a pot of coffee, and points the browser for the corporate network. The director uses the *Times'* Web-based system to manage performance and capacity of all aspects of a 6000-node local area network and a wide area network that has 26 sites.

"Just about every day, I fire up the browser and view the reports from the previous day," the director says. That way, when the director gets to the office, there are no surprises awaiting. If there have been any incidents overnight, the director is aware of the situation before leaving for the office. If the alarms should be critical, the director can grab a phone and contact the correct members of the team to get them working on the situation as soon as they hit the office.

IS managers trying to provide ample bandwidth to users often find that limitations in their network management systems mean that unpleasant surprises await them when they sit down to their consoles at the beginning of the workday. Often, it can be a major time-consumer to drill down into the network's performance statistics or to try to set up a long-term look at a particular portion of the network.

The *Times'* director has no such problems. Using Concord's Network Health, the director is able to go back and look at performance five minutes, five hours, or five days before an incident. "Otherwise," the director notes, "You have to manage from the point the problem was reported forward."

While security issues have been addressed in depth, the director actually invites people at the *Times* to go ahead and poke around in the performance statistics. The network gives read-only access to statistics and performance. However, this very feature allows senior management and other communities of interest to have access to performance metrics. "It's no longer a black box to the customer," the director says.

If that seems like smart management to you, it is. But another New York City–based organization has gone beyond smart managers and smart management to using Web-based management to run smart buildings.

Trump Moves to Smart Buildings

The Trump Organization in New York City is also among those benefiting from the flexibility of Web-based management. It calls its project the *Smart Building* initiative. Under an agreement with XS Bandwidth of Alexandria, Louisiana, Trump is wiring the Trump Towers, Trump Plaza, and 200 other commercial and residential buildings for a variety of services, including video-on-demand and Internet service. The entire system is monitored and managed over the Internet from XS's location in Louisiana. Figure 5.2 demonstrates a typical multi-tenant construct.

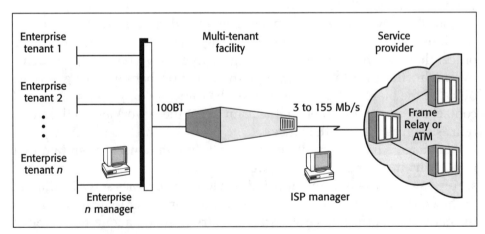

Figure 5.2   Multitenant Internet access.

Source: Xedia Corporation

The operations director for XS uses HP's OpenView to monitor and a custom-developed in-house management tool to manage the network. Among the components managed in the network are Xedia Access Point for managed bandwidth services, Amati DSL devices, Cabletron's 6000-series department-level switches, N-Cube video-on-demand, DEC's Alpha products for e-mail and similar applications, and routing via Cisco's 7000-series products. Many Trump-owned offices are being wired to support local area network backbones. At the same time, carriers are bringing their fiber and broadband services infrastructure directly into the facilities. The two dynamics have created the opportunity to deliver high-speed Internet access to a centrally managed point in the building.

In addition to its own program, XS uses Access Point from Xedia to manage the bandwidth sent to each individual building tenant. Given that it expects to expand to five more cities in the next two years, XS is looking at packaged Internet-based management products such as Computer Associates' Total Enterprise Management package and Cabletron's SPECTRUM.

Keep in mind that there are a lot of Web-based management package choices available. Some of those choices go beyond simple network analysis allowing you to drive your management programs off into other areas as well.

Racing to the Future

There are Web-based monitoring applications that promise to take data monitoring down a different road. In fact, Formula One motor racing and high-performance computing have come together in a big way thanks to a management system of a different kind. West McLaren Mercedes of Woking, England, one of the world's most successful racing teams, wants to win every race, and it is using software—along with motor oil and skilled mechanics—to achieve its mission.

The Real World Interface from Computer Associates, Inc. (CA), analyzes critical Formula One performance measures on the West McLaren Mercedes car, such as the impact of front and rear brake pressure on speed. Under this innovative technology partnership, West McLaren Mercedes and CA are developing a comprehensive solution that gives the racing team's engineers the ability to easily assess and analyze the Formula One MP4/12 car's performance—including everything from throttle response to the g forces exerted on the driver when going around a circuit.

McLaren's managing director notes that because of the high costs associated with Grand Prix racing, everyone in the team is driven to achieve perfection, meaning that everything must be accomplished in the most efficient manner possible, under the most extreme pressure. Processing data and information through modern information technology techniques is absolutely essential to the efficient running of the organization.

The analytical power for the system is supplied by sophisticated manager/agent technology, which interfaces with West McLaren Mercedes' data acquisition systems. Software agents monitor critical functions on the Formula One MP4/12 car, collecting performance and operational data from the vehicle's telemetry system. The analysis includes critical Formula One performance measures such as engine rpm correlated against throttle opening.

Telemetry monitoring of Formula One cars is not new. The technology will bring to the track a synergistic view of performance data. The engineers can compare critical data to identify causal relationships. For instance, they can use the three-dimensional display of the car to see how different brake setups affect g forces, or how engine rpms correlate against the throttle. Data collected from previous races is available for comparison to improve the competitiveness of the car.

Can we treat a high-performance network the same way these Formula One racers treat their cars? Why not? Look for data-gathering and monitoring efforts in other nontraditional endeavors to slide over into computing soon, and vice versa.

The Next Wave

While it is good to know about the possibilities and potential of Web-based management systems, it is best to keep both feet planted firmly on the ground while dealing with today's networking challenges.

It is the standard applications—such as those used by the utilities, ImageNation, and the *New York Times*—that constitute the core future of Web-based management.

In the next chapter we take a peek around the corner at what to expect in future generations of products. And, rather than go off far into the future, we will keep our feet firmly planted on what to expect within our business lifetimes—the next several years.

Where SNMP and RMON Fit with Web-Based Management

It is not a big step to see how almost any enterprise with multiple locations or multiple networks could end up taking advantage of Web-based network management. There is something in the concept of Web-based management for almost everyone. There is some work involved, as well. Call it the price of admission. One of the requirements is understanding some of the protocols that are involved.

SNMP, its offspring RMON and RMON2, HTML, and HTTP are among the keys to knowing what is going on in network management and in the world of today's workstation-based management platforms which may or may not use the Internet. Regardless of whether your organization is involved in any of these areas, it is still a good idea to be up-to-date on the other pieces of the puzzle.

RMON is a simple network management protocol (SNMP) used to manage networks remotely. The key to RMON (SNMP's *remote monitoring* specification) is its ability to allow interoperability between monitoring devices or management terminals from a variety of vendors. RMON probes are basically dedicated RMON agents on the network. RMON provides the information required to establish the boundaries between collision domains (LAN switches) and broadcast domains (routers).

RMON probes often serve as a sort of "passport" on a Web-based systems trip through the network. The more segmented a LAN is, the more important it is to be able to drill down into the network and see what is going on in a switched or LAN-based network. Ethernet-based LANs typically require the most analysis and tracking across nodes. RMON allows the network manager to provide a logical boundary between the collision and broadcast domains.

There are two RMONs in common use. The original RMON operates at the media access control (MAC) level (that is, the collision domain). It is defined by Request for Comment (RFC) 1757. The newer RMON2 operates at the network level and higher up the stack. Keep in mind that RMON agents gather physical- and data-link-layer data for a single LAN segment. Meanwhile, RMON2 agents collect data at the network and application layers for analysis of flows between parts of the enterprise network. It is the combination of RMON and RMON2 agents that provides a network manager with detailed information about any LAN segment as well as end-to-end traffic analysis across complex networks.

Typically, a network manager will use a management station to interface with a manageable device such as a switch or router. Within the device is a management information base (MIB) which stores information on a set of statistics. The protocol (say, SNMP) facilitates the conversation between the station and the device. The feature that differentiates RMON from SNMP is its use of additional MIB groups. Included in the RFC (a list of elements proposed for standardization) are nine additional statistical groups for Ethernet. RMON-capable devices can gather extended MIB data in addition to that provided by SNMP and then sort and summarize the results. This allows a deeper and more specific analysis of data traffic and also reduces management overhead through limited polling and transmission intervals.

The good news about SNMP (and RMON, by extension) is that it does work. The bad news is that, although the Internet Engineering Task Force (IETF) has put together standards for SNMP, there are many vendors who have developed their own MIB (SNMP's management information base) to work along with the standard MIB definitions. The rival to SNMP is open systems interconnection (OSI). But SNMP has several advantages, not the least of which is that a whole lot of vendors are using SNMP today. A lot of people like SNMP. In this business, it's hard to hate anything whose first name is *Simple*. From the vendor's point of view, SNMP also is a relatively cheap route to take.

The RMON MIB brings additional packet error counters, historic trend graphing and statistical analysis, traffic matrixes, threshold and alarm

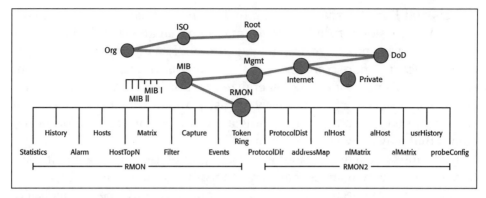

Figure 6.1 RMON/RMON2 MIB tree.
Source: Bay Networks

information, and filters that capture and analyze individual packets (Figure 6.1). RMON agents are intelligent, carrying out assigned collection tasks without further supervision. They can detect conditions that require further attention and report them to remote management centers. Local processing at the collection point is especially important in the wide area environment; transferring raw data in bulk is expensive and adds to congestion. Intelligence also allows for local actions governed by administrative policies. For example, an RMON agent may detect a broadcast storm on a switch port and alert other local elements. These elements may carry out a policy that disables the port until staff can investigate.

As another example, an RMON2 agent may identify the stations that are using a specific server application and communicate that information to a management tool that automatically configures an application-based virtual LAN (VLAN).

Although there are other, more elegant management systems (many are object-oriented), such as CMIP, CMISE, and the like, SNMP is like the proverbial camel: SNMP and its RMON suites have their noses in the network management tent. It's going to be tough to keep the rest of the camel out.

SNMP MIBs

Although SNMP itself is relatively simple, it takes some work to build the MIB support in an agent, and considerably more work to build the management support to utilize the MIB data, and a great deal of work to deploy the manager onto the various network management platforms. Chris

Wellers and Karl Auerbach, writing in *The Simple Times* (December 1997), an open discussion forum for SNMP, maintain that an HTTP/HTML management server embedded in a managed device, with underlying TCP, is not significantly more complex or memory intensive than an SNMP agent with mechanisms supporting generalized lexi-ordering and arbitrary collections of objects in a SET. It is easy to vastly underestimate the amount of work required for an agent to handle an arbitrary collection of proposed values that may arrive in a SET request.

If one looks at many of today's workstation-based management platforms, one quickly realizes that they are really not much more than a collection of device-specific add-ons. Those add-ons could be just as easily created by having a device export highly device specific Web pages with controls and user-interface paradigms. For example, management platforms take pride in the fact that they can project a rendering of a managed device, so that the operator can point at a port to invoke a control panel for that specific port. This is pretty routine stuff for a typical Web server. The device vendor ships one self-contained product. That product includes its own management functions and does not depend on anything except that Web browsers are reasonably uniform and ubiquitous. With respect to its management functions, the vendor controls the horizontal and it controls the vertical—the vendor controls everything about the device and its management, from operation to GUI. It's an extremely attractive proposition.

The great drawback of this approach is that it requires human intelligence to comprehend the Web forms presented by a device. If one accepts the proposition, as the author does, that in the long term networks should perform significant self-management, then this approach represents a substantial danger that we will end up further from our goal rather than closer.

SNMP should not be confused as being network management, Wellers and Auerbach state. Rather, SNMP is merely an access method used by a management station to read and write items in an agent's MIB. Today's Internet is successfully carrying an enormous transaction load using the World Wide Web's HTTP, which is a TCP-based protocol. HTTP transactions follow a simple life cycle:

1. Client creates a TCP connection to the server.

2. Client transmits an HTTP operation, usually a GET or a POST, to the server. Although both can be used to carry additional information from the client to the server, POST has no restrictions on the size or structure of that information.

3. The server responds with an HTTP header followed by a Multipurpose Internet Mail Extension–(MIME-) typed chunk of binary data of

arbitrary size. This data may be literally anything that can be reduced to binary. It may be the familiar HTML of Web pages, a JPEG image, or instructions to the browser on how to launch a multicast backbone (MBONE) viewer.

4. The connection is closed.

Much effort is being expended to rectify HTTP's major shortcoming: It does not do enough work per TCP connection. Efforts are underway to reduce this weakness.

Consider SNMP queries as the equivalent of a Web form in which the user or management station simply lists the MIB objects it wants to obtain or set values into. The SNMP response would be the Web page returned as a result of processing the input form. For processing efficiency, this result need not be encoded in a way that could be directly presented to a human user. The data could be handled either by a special application that speaks HTTP or by a management plug-in to a Web browser. One very attractive feature about the approach outlined by Wellers and Auerbach is that it may be able to piggyback on those Web security features that are falling into place. The main drawback of the scheme is that it can be highly intensive in its use of TCP connections, but as has been mentioned, the Web community is already facing and, hopefully, resolving this problem.

How One Vendor Handles HTTP

Hypertext Transfer Protocol (HTTP) is the primary transfer protocol used by the World Wide Web. The HTTP model is an extremely simple one. The typical transaction is one in which the client establishes a connection to the server, issues a request, and waits for a response from the server. The server, upon receiving the request from the client, processes the client's request, sends a response, and then closes the connection.

HTTP is a platform-independent document description language. The language is a subset of Standard Generalized Markup Language (SGML), which is a more elaborate ISO document standard. (This should sound familiar to SNMP people.) HTML was designed to be used over low-bandwidth communications links. Ironically, this makes it ideally suited for exporting formatted information from management agents, which are generally embedded systems. As Patrick Mullaney of Cabletron, writing in *The Simple Times* (July 1996), points out, the general philosophy of the language is not to control every aspect of the display. Through the language, the page designer gives hints to the display station as to the layout of a page; it avoids the overhead of controlling every aspect of the display down to the pixel level. This minimizes the amount of information that needs to be transferred to display a particular resource (i.e., a document). This lack of complexity gives HTML, regardless of the particular document, its familiar look and feel and ease of operation.

Proper page design philosophy has been to minimize bandwidth used by minimizing the amount of information a document contains (image content in particular). This philosophy also benefits management agents, which generally don't have a large amount of persistent storage, by requiring them to store only a minimum of information at the agent.

HTML uses markup tags to denote regions of text as having specific characteristics. The tags serve as instructions to the browser on how to render a region of text. These tags are portions of text surrounded by the less-than (<) and greater-than (>) characters. For example, the <B> tag indicates that the browser should bold the text following the tag and a </B> indicates to the browser that the bolding should end. HTML provides tags for the formatting of text, inclusion of graphic images, navigation to other documents (hyperlinks), and standard form controls (text boxes, radio buttons, and so on).

The Web-based agent implementation described in this section exports HTML-formatted management documents to a standard Web browser. No specialized management station software is needed to use the agent. There are three issues to consider: (1) document design, (2) agent implementation, and (3) authentication.

Cabletron's Web-based management agent has three distinct classes of documents:

1. The *static document* is a document whose contents never change. It can be built into the agent in the form of a static data structure, put in the agent's persistent storage, or referenced by the agent by using a URL naming a supporting device (a supporting server or another agent). Examples of static documents are graphic images, help or informational documents, and HTML documents used entirely for the user's navigation to other documents (via hyperlinks).

2. The *dynamic document's* contents have the potential to change over time. The contents of a dynamic document are assembled at run-time upon a request for the document from the client. This is the most common type of document supported by Cabletron's agent. It can be used for many purposes, such as dynamically displaying the current values of statistics kept at the agent and the current values of user-configurable operational parameters at the agent.

3. The *form document* is used to modify the current operational mode of the device or agent. Form documents can be either static or dynamic themselves. The controls (e.g., textbox submission fields, two-state buttons, or multichoice selection boxes) on forms often have current state values associated with them. These state values must be inserted into the control upon a request for the form document.

The layout of documents for Cabletron's agent is done with the aid of a commercially available HTML layout editor. This tool is augmented by a tool developed in-house that gives the document designer the ability to associate certain fields within a document with dynamic (or live) data within the device and, in the case of form documents, supply an action method for each control element to be executed upon form submission.

Once the HTML document has been designed, a code generator is run on the document to generate supporting code and data structures (as a C++ class). The supporting code consists of methods for registering the document with the agent, the document name method, the document serialization method, the document authentication realm method, and, for a form document, a method for processing the control elements submitted in a POST request. The registration method simply adds the document to a directory of documents maintained by the agent. This directory is simply a data structure used to hold and retrieve documents by name (Request-URI). Upon a request from a client, the agent searches the directory using the Request-URI as a key to find a particular document. For a GET request, the document's serialization method is called when the agent receives a request for the document. The results of the serialization method are the current contents of the document. These results are returned as the data section of the HTTP response.

In the case of a POST request, the document's serialization routine is called after the document has processed the data section of the request. The document's control element parsing method separates the data section of the request into control/value pairs. Each pair represents the submitted value of a specific control on the form. Then, for each control, the parsing method calls a specific user-supplied method (defined in the document design step), passing the value associated with the control. The serialization results for a form after processing a POST method is completely up to the form designer. The results could simply be the form document with the new values used in the form submission, or be a document indicating the success or failure of the submission.

The agent itself can be configured to be single- or multithreaded. The advantage of using a multithreaded server is primarily increased throughput. For many management implementations, a singly threaded server is fine. (Browsing a Web-based management agent isn't particularly exciting!)

Another advantage of a multithreaded agent is that when it is used with persistent connections, the agent will be able to service more than one client at a time. Persistent connections are aimed at solving the latency problem with TCP slow-start. Persistent connections were added ad hoc in HTTP 1.0 and will become standard in HTTP 1.1. The disadvantages are possible manager conflict and resource consumption issues.

The Cabletron agent uses two authentication realms (protection spaces) within the device: read-only and read-write. The agent maintains two passwords, one for read-only access and one for read-write access, which are stored in persistent storage on the device. (This is quite similar to SNMP, and on some Cabletron devices, the SNMP community strings will be used as the passwords). A read-only password allows the client (browser) to access pages only in the read-only realm. The read-write password allows access to both realms.

Each document in Cabletron's agent is associated with one realm. If a client fails to authenticate itself with the agent for a particular document, the agent challenges the client with that document's realm (read-only or read-write). The agent can determine a document's realm using the document's authentication realm method, which simply returns a string indicating the realm. In Cabletron's implementation, informational documents typically require only a read-only level of access, but may occasionally require read-write if they contain privileged information. Form documents are generally not accessible at the read-only level of access.

RMON at the Core

Many vendors, like 3Com, see RMON as an integral part of the entire Web-based management system. 3Com's Transcend Traffix Manager for Windows NT provides a desktop-to-WAN visualization of enterprise traffic to help network managers better understand the impact of application deployment throughout the network. It collects and correlates data from standard RMON and RMON2 probes and embedded agents, providing a global view of network traffic for performance management, trend analysis, and troubleshooting. Through its highly intuitive GUI, it can quickly and easily drill down to every host and data stream in the network, allowing managers to more easily monitor and enforce corporate network usage policies.

RMON and RMON2 actually give a network manager much the same information that would be expected from an advanced, intelligent protocol analyzer. In addition, a manager can set up thresholds and provide alarms when the thresholds underperform or are exceeded, can set trigger points for automatic changes when certain events occur, and can do other basic, proactive management tasks.

In a 1994 study on Remote Network Monitoring, McConnell Consulting of Boulder, Colorado, found using RMON increased management staff effectiveness by allowing them to manage more segments per staff member compared to organizations that do not use RMON. Further, Figure 1.3 on page 10 shows the savings in staffing costs between those who use RMON and those who do not, with managed environments of equal size used for comparison.

RMON probes give a manager a huge amount of information on the performance being attained in the network, as well as a look at traffic patterns and what is going on with individual protocol performance. As more and more networks go to a switched topology (rather than relying on bridges and routers), the results of RMON testing can let the engineer do proactive testing by examining the network statistics for any abnormality. A decent RMON setup will pinpoint utilization patterns that exceed the design thresholds for the network. Best of all, RMON will allow the engineers to provide bounding between the MAC collision domain and the broadcast, or IP/ARP, domain. Of course, all of this is done remotely. The RMON MIB agents work on a variety of intermediate devices like bridges, routers, switches, hubs, and dedicated or nondedicated hosts.

The goal of a company like 3Com is to deliver end-to-end management of 3Com network systems, simplify and automate network operations, increase reliability, and reduce the total cost of network ownership. As each new version of a product comes out, vendors see themselves as taking a step closer to enabling users to manage their network as a business resource rather than an office tool. A typical lifecycle model is shown in Figure 6.2.

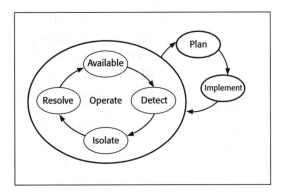

Figure 6.2 Network management lifecycle model.

Source: Bay Networks, Inc./Netsation

RMON has been around for a long time—at least since 1989 as part of the SNMP suite. The first specific RMON specification was developed about five years later as RFC 1271. There are 10 RMON groups defined in RFC 1757:

1. Statistics group.
2. History group.
3. Alarm group.
4. Host group.
5. Host TopN group.
6. Traffic matrix group.
7. Filter group.
8. Packet capture group.
9. Event group.
10. Token ring group.

RMON2 is oriented to collecting information about application- and network-layer protocol communication patterns. Under RMON2, several new groups have been added to the RMON capability. They include a network- and application-layer *host* that gives statistics on packets received for Layer 3 (as well as Layer 2) traffic; network- and applications-layer *matrix*, for statistics at the network and applications layer between source and destination nodes on the network; *protocol directory*, which is a user-selected suite of protocols to be monitored; *protocol distribution*, which handles the statistics gathered for each protocol in the protocol directory; *user-definable history*, which will sample any MIB object monitored by the RMON agent; *address mapping*, which lists the MAC- to network-layer addresses; and the *configuration group*, which gives RMON agent configurations and capabilities. Today the number of RMON users is growing into areas like mixing the use of hub-based embedded probe-agents with stand-alone probes. Some use RMON-based data for additional analysis in conjunction with other types of data from the network. There are also changes in RMON-like management, including RMON-like data collection, which is now being applied to other media such as FDDI; other parts of the Enterprise network, including the WAN; and new environments, including Ethernet, Token Ring, and asynchronous transfer mode (ATM) switches.

There also are Unix RMON utilities, based on Remote Monitoring Standard RFC 1757. They are available as a stand-alone suite of programs (with its own launch program), or integrated with common UNIX management applications such as HP OpenView, SunNet Manager, or IBM's Netview 6000.

An RMON application sets the appropriate MIB variables to specify measurement intervals, thresholds, and other operational parameters. The agent collects and stores information and delivers it to the remote client on request. Agents also send an SNMP trap when specified conditions have been detected, thereby alerting a remote client about a situation requiring immediate attention.

Some older devices—and even some more recent products, especially those that are non-IP products—do not include network management agents and can not communicate with SNMP management devices except through echo packets. RMON MIB agents monitor every network device. They often are the only way to extend network management to devices which otherwise could not be managed.

Maintaining network availability and assuring quality of service is the network administrator's prime responsibility. Remote agents facilitate these tasks by providing faster, real-time response to problems because no travel time is wasted. This directly translates into higher availability and better service quality. Further savings result because staff members need not be permanently at a LAN segment in order to speed responses to outages. In addition, the agent is already in place and has substantial intelligence, allowing automatic initiation of diagnostic measurements when specified conditions are detected on that LAN segment, McConnell says.

The agent offers strong value for tactical management—detecting problems, identifying causes, and maintaining high availability and quality. "Network administrators are always struggling to create a proactive management environment; one in which problems are anticipated and corrected before they have any substantial impact on the community of users and on the organization's ability to carry out its business activities. Continuous monitoring gives network administrators a new opportunity to move in this direction," McConnell says in *The Simple Times* (July 1996). For example, collected information can be used to build activity baselines defining the normal behavior of any given LAN segment. Administrators are alerted when network behaviors are out of the normal range and they can head off problems before they are noticed by the users.

Characterizing the behavior of complex internetworks is a challenge. For example, a problem between a client on one segment and a server across the campus involves several LAN segments with their own traffic loads. Information from a set of RMON2 agents can be correlated to give a deeper understanding of the traffic flowing between segments. New agents provide information about traffic flows between subnetworks, the distribution of protocol traffic, and applications activity.

The filtering abilities of RMON2 agents allow even finer levels of granularity. For example, packets can be filtered on criteria such as protocol type or application usage, providing a highly detailed look at individual conversations across the LAN segment.

The most complete testing of RMON data readily available can be found by contacting the University of New Hampshire's InterOperability Lab. It can be accessed at www.iol.unh.edu/index.html.

A Ph.D.'s Comparison of Options

The rapid growth of computer networks and the increasing reliance on these networks to run mission critical applications has created a strong correlation between end-user perspective of application response time and business productivity. IT managers are seeking quality of service (QoS) assurances from their service providers so that the end user can access application servers efficiently. As a result, service providers are seeking monitoring tools for application response time from the internetworking vendors so that the customer can receive consistent and verifiable application service.

According to Erfan Ibrahim, Ph.D., with Jyra Research, Inc., of San Jose, California, internetworking vendors are in turn developing application response-time monitoring capabilities into their network management products or partnering with third-party software vendors who already have such tools in the market. The key challenge is to incorporate enough features in the monitoring tool to make it useful for the service provider but not overwhelm them in cost and management complexity, he says.

Application response time can be measured by embedded probes or external agents placed around the network. Embedded probes can be of two types: *SNMP-based* using proprietary MIBs embedded in hubs, routers, or switches; and *promiscuous packet monitoring* software embedded in the client desktop.

Ibrahim also divides external agents into two camps: *Java agents* attached to user segments running synthetic transactions and *promiscuous packet monitoring agents* attached to user segments. Depending on the customer need, each approach has its benefits and challenges. He lists the following as the strengths of each approach:

SNMP-Based Solution Benefits (example: Cisco IPM/RTR)

- Requires no stand-alone data collection tool.

- Management and configuration are built into the network management platform.

- Proprietary MIB gives the internetworking vendor greater flexibility in choice of application support.

- Provides a low-cost solution.

- Remote deployment is possible.

Client-Desktop-Based Packet Monitoring Software Benefits (example: Vital Suite by Vital Signs)

- Gives most accurate measure of end-user application response time.

- Able to monitor response times of several application protocols simultaneously from the desktop.

- Provides alarming capability to the end user and IT manager for applications that respond too slowly.

- Provides a low-cost solution, no additional hardware is required.

- Captures anomalies in end-user application response time.

- Remote deployment is possible.

Java-Based External Agents Benefits (example: Jyra Research Service Management Architecture)

- Collects relevant data to monitor service-level agreements (SLAs) at an enterprise level.

- Gives average response-time measurement from end-user segments.

- Synthetic transactions give round-the-clock measurement of application response time.

- Independent of end-user usage profile.

- Distributed directory structure allows business-centric reporting capability.

- Causes no impact on end-user systems.

- Provides alarming and thresholding capability to the IT manager for SLA violations.

- Provides scalable architecture for data collection, summarization, and reporting.

Promiscuous Packet Monitoring External Agents Benefits (example: Ecoscope by Compuware)

- Provides multiapplication monitoring capability.

- Causes no impact on end-user systems.

- Scalable to high-speed links.

- Provides alarming capability to IT manager for applications that respond too slowly.

- Causes no impact on network performance.

Given the pros and cons of the many features offered by a variety of vendors, Ibrahim makes the following recommendations for each type of solution.

The ideal customer for an SNMP-based solution would be an enterprise or service provider that requires basic response-time monitoring capability of application servers without the breakdown of the application transaction time (i.e., HTTP server TCP connect time, download page time, download images time, etc.). Furthermore, these customers do not require collection of response time from many applications or multiple sites and do not demand the end-user perspective of application response time. These customers also require that this basic functionality be given at minimal incremental cost. Such customers maintain service-level agreements on the availability of application servers at the TCP layer.

Ibrahim's research shows that the ideal customer for client-desktop-based packet monitoring software would be an enterprise that wants to place the responsibility of application monitoring on the end user and does not require that the response-time statistics be gathered for summary reporting for service-level agreements. Such customers do not want to incur any incremental hardware cost or network management resources. Typically, these customers are either small in size or have not developed service-level agreements with third-party service providers.

The ideal network suited to Java-based external agents would be a service provider that is offering Web hosting, DNS, and database services to its end customers. Large enterprises such as Fortune 1000 companies would also be a good candidate for this solution. The key differentiator for this target market is the need for comprehensive application response-time monitoring (i.e., detailed application transaction time breakdown) and reporting capability with business-centric reporting that is scalable, reliable, accurate, and affordable.

These customers have, or are in the process of setting up, sophisticated service-level agreements internally and/or externally and require a powerful application response-time monitoring tool that has visibility in the network layer as well as the application layer. These customers are also very dependent on short application response time for their profitability and are therefore willing to expend monetary resources to obtain a verifiable SLA tool.

Promiscuous packet monitoring external agents are an ideal solution for enterprises looking for a high endpoint solution to monitor key links in their networks. Such customers have invoked SLAs in limited parts of their networks and are looking for a low-cost solution to monitor the traffic of key end users, Ibrahim says. These customers also have highly impacted systems and want a stand-alone monitoring capability to avoid adverse effects on their end-user systems and internetworking devices. There is no panacea for application response-time monitoring. However, no solution can survive in the market in the long run unless it addresses the following customer concerns:

- Multiapplication support
- Reliability
- Accuracy
- Affordability

As SLAs become more prominent in the day-to-day management of networks, customers will seek tools that can provide a verifiable measurement of application response time more from a business perspective and less from the traditional device- or server-centric view prevalent in most network monitoring tools today.

Keep in mind that Java-based external agents require additional hardware and support, and longer lead times for developing new application support. Additional expenses will be incurred for software, and any anomalies in the end user's perspective of application response time will not be captured.

The Future of Web-Based Systems

As long as one buys into the idea that the Internet, Internet-2, IP-based networking, or corporate intranets will continue to be part of the networking schemes of the twenty-first century, then there is not a doubt in the world that browser-based network management systems will continue to flourish in the marketplace.

In fact, some say the Web could end the quest for the universal console. Today, management consoles and applications are wed to servers, use proprietary APIs, and contain proprietary tools such as scripting languages. This makes customizing solutions even tougher; the best you can hope for in many cases is that applications run without crashing each other. But system integrators and in-house developers can leverage Web development skills to create custom management consoles that can be integrated with online help databases and other in-house tools in ways that haven't been possible with dedicated management consoles.

Not surprisingly, management vendors have been rushing to Web-enable products. Standards have begun to emerge in the Web-based management arena. It's clear that the move to Web-based management is well under way, and it will change things for the better. So, when you're planning your intranet, remember to give equal time to planning the management infrastructure you'll create as a part of that intranet.

A quick glance at the corporate vendors shows that a list of giant firms such as AT&T, Cabletron, Hewlett-Packard, INRANGE Technologies, IBM, and Sun are on the Web-based management bandwagon. Web-based management is here to stay. The number of smaller firms involved shows that there is a veritable algae bloom of ideas on expanding and improving Web-based management in the future. In any environment in which both the giants and the smaller fry are flourishing, the outlook is excellent for the continued growth and expansion of the market.

The vision for many firms using Web-based management and producing the tools is not one of Web-based *network* management, but, rather, Web-based *enterprise* management. Any device or tool that would hurt the corporation if its performance was limited is a target for Web-based management. Little by little, the constraints encountered today will fade.

"Businesses are recognizing that poor service quality is a major contributor to reduced productivity and lost revenues. Effective service-level management requires integrated management of the transport, computing and applications infrastructures," according to McConnell Consulting of Boulder, Colorado. "All three must be managed end-to-end and incorporate products from a variety of vendors."

Web-based management will expand. There are at least five directions in which it will grow, and probably more:

1. More powerful tools.
2. More ubiquitous deployment of those tools.
3. Use of the tools deeper into the corporate structure.
4. Tools for specialty or proprietary products.
5. Ancillary tools to support Web-based management.

The first category is a given. Already most of the corporations covered in this book have their next-generation products ready to come out of the development labs. Whether it is a second-generation tool, or an advancement on Version 5.0, it proves that the people who are putting their corporate futures and their money at risk see a continuation of a broad-based market for Web-based management tools.

There are several separate areas in which Web-based network management can (and will) progress. An advance in any one of those areas will put pressure on other areas to move forward. The result will be a sort of reverse death-spiral: The entire technology will advance every time one segment moves forward.

Among the key areas to keep up with are Web-based reporting and statistics, Web-based systems administration, Web-based management platforms, and Web-based management tools. The interplay of all of these areas will spell the future of Web-based network management.

One key area will be bringing Web-based management tools into the managed devices themselves. While every manufacturer is making scalable, seamless, integrated products, NetOps of Pleasantville, New York, is looking for the product that includes embedded early-stage fault detection. The router itself would use the Web to call out to the network manager, "Come check me!" In addition to the infrastructure area, NetOps sees two other places where embedded proactive help would be a value to the network manager and to the vendor. The first is in the leading enterprise platform products such as Tivoli, NetView, Unicenter, and OpenView. Many of them are working in that direction today. The other market target is the service provider segment. In fact, NetOps is working with AT&T Solutions in this area today.

Neural Agents

Web-based management is a powerful tool. But what if the management system could go a step beyond reporting what is going on in the network and recognize patterns that could be potentially harmful to the network? Look for an increasing number of vendors to include neural network agents in their products.

Neural agents are the answer to a common network manager's complaint: "I've got so much information coming in here already, what do I want with something else that's going to give me more detail, more reports on nodes, more stuff to deal with? I can't handle what I have!"

Neural agents are designed to answer just that problem. They can be viewed as low-cost technical assistants. They poke out through the network and begin to recognize and record patterns of use in the network. Once the neural agent "learns" that a certain pattern exists (and confirms its belief by discovering it numerous times), it will warn the technician that there is a potential situation that will arise in the future if not remedied now. Neural agents are quite flexible and can be applied almost anywhere, from the application level to the network, server, or client levels. They go far beyond the simple identification of a problem (say, transmitting a yellow warning when traffic on a certain segment exceeds 85 percent of capacity, with the hope that someone will rectify the problem before the problem gets into the red zone). True neural agents actually look at the statistical probability of an event occurring. In other words, the neural agent may learn that every time the network polls the Louisville office at the same time that another office is transmitting data, usage exceeds a given threshold. While it might not recognize that the reason for the conflict is that all Kentucky offices upload through Louisville, it will tell the network manager that there is a high likelihood that the network will crash if the manager continues to proceed in this manner.

The neural agent may also learn that the conflict occurs only when other events are in place: Perhaps it happens only on Fridays, or happens only when a session is in place after 3 P.M. Whatever the underlying cause, the neural agent takes much of the demand for predictive, accurate data analysis off the shoulders of the network manager and puts them back into the management system where they belong. However, it well behooves the network manager to pay attention to the neural agent when it sounds a warning.

Linking a neural agent with Web-based technology gives management a variety of options for delivering such warnings and for implementing change or remediation when the time comes.

From Trial to Implementation

It is fair to say that once a user organization gets its feet wet with Web-based management, the use of browser-based tools will expand. In many cases, the use of Web-based management is limited to a single application area, a single geographic area, or a limited set of business sectors where the tools were used as a trial. The success of these trials bodes well for the expanded deployment of Web-based tools. Pilot programs typically have been used where the MIS or IT department felt it could most benefit from an application. Perhaps the application was monitoring a single remote location. Perhaps it was bringing a number of similar sites under control—an application where a central corporate insurance company headquarters needed to provide management of many local agencies' computing facilities. Perhaps it was a "toy" or a trial for one individual who was interested in seeing how Web-based management would work in a particular scenario. In any case, successful implementation in one area will lead to successful expansion into other areas.

Device vendors are usually under pressure to deliver their products to the market quickly. However, as previously noted, in addition to developing the device itself, the vendor is required to develop the agent software and a management application. The current NMS architecture of a framework plus applications offers substantial power to device vendors in order to develop sophisticated management applications. But the first problem a device vendor faces is having to learn the APIs provided by the framework, engineers at Wipro point out. An added problem is that these APIs have not been standardized. Therefore, management applications are not portable across frameworks.

As a result, a device vendor typically decides on one particular framework and develops the management application on top of that framework. Device customers are then required to purchase that specific framework and the management application. If a customer has two devices from two different vendors, and the corresponding management applications run on two different frameworks, the customer has to purchase the two frameworks, and possibly two different workstations to run them. In addition, the network administrator at the customer's site is required to learn how to use both network management systems.

Device customers are generally reluctant to accept these terms. A customer may have a favorite NMS framework and will pressure device vendors to develop management applications to run on that framework. Vendors resist this pressure because it is both expensive and time-consuming for them to develop applications on each framework.

In addition, some device vendors target low-price markets, where their customers may not be willing to purchase an expensive framework and an associated high-end workstation. These device vendors typically develop a stand-alone management application. Although a stand-alone application may be harder to build, it can be built to run on less expensive hardware.

These tools will be used deeper in the corporate structure. Everyone expects top management to be given access to view telephone and Internet usage statistics and costs for everyone in the organization. However, the future of Web-based management and reporting puts that information into the hands of any approved supervisor or other manager—from any spot where an IP-based computer can be accessed, at any hour of the day or night. The chief benefit is that these managers can spot abnormal usage and associated costs quickly and easily. While chargeback is a key issue for telephone usage, IT managers are concerned with abnormal Internet usage:

- How are employees accessing the Internet?

- When are employees accessing the Internet?

- How long are they staying online?

- What are they doing when they are there?

- Are they accessing sites that are potentially embarrassing to the company or to fellow workers?

- Is the department getting the level of service it is supposed to get while hooked to the corporate intranet?

- Does a department's usage of the Internet justify further bandwidth allocation?

Some vendors believe that the IP-PBX will probably be the next device with which systems will have to integrate. Feeding ISP billing systems may be another potential growth area for telemanagement systems.

There is considerable activity on extending the scope and capabilities of the Web. Work is being done on extending the HTTP protocol and in defining new standards for the same. Individual browser vendors such as Netscape are beginning to support a number of extensions to HTTP and HTML to make access to Web pages faster and to make Web pages more attractive. The introduction of the Java language and the Java run-time system enable Web pages to incorporate little programs (called *applets*) that can be downloaded from the server and executed on the browser. Using Java applets, alarms may be sounded in case a fault is detected. In an era of standards and simplicity, low cost will play a significant role in determining the success of new management models. The potential of Java has been widely recognized in the industry, with many software and hardware vendors expressing interest in the technology. Virtual Reality Markup Language (VRML) is another page representation that is beginning to become popular, because it offers the ability to represent and manipulate three-dimensional objects. The more that Web technology evolves over the next few years, the more features will be available for remote and Web-based management.

Gathering information, compiling it in a convenient and useful form, being able to analyze the information or automate the automation process, and providing secure access or handily distributing it to the people who want it in a timely fashion all are key components to the future success of Web-based management. If the cult of computer priests has learned one thing in the past decade, it should be that management will not tolerate information hoarding. Face it: Nobody other than other technology freaks really cares how the computer does its job, whether it accesses information over the Web, whether it is distributed over an intranet or over the Internet, whether the IS department is using version 2.6 or 2.7. What they want is relevant information *now.* If it is convenient to access, if they can pull it down with a simple bookmark and their browser, so much the better.

This is where Web-based management tools will score over the existing proprietary models. Engineers at Wipro maintain that in a one-on-one comparison, the benefits of Web-based management are so compelling that even the most ardent fan of proprietary management tools will be able to see them, thereby ushering in a new era.

Enterprise management vendors are under tremendous amounts of pressure not only to increase the functionality and scope of their products, but also to decrease product complexity. Mainframe reliability levels are being demanded in a distributed and heterogeneous world. As the Yankee Group of Boston, Massachusetts, notes, this means that administrators need additional tools and features to make themselves more productive and to find problems long before they occur. Otherwise, the demand for reliability becomes untenable. Many lessons have already been learned from the rapidly evolving enterprise management market. Yankee Group points to the fact that an appealing graphical user interface (GUI) means nothing if the data is not fully integrated tightly at the back end, and tight integration at the back end is of little use without a front end that displays all relationships in an intuitive way.

In between, of course, is the vital linking of the back end and the front end. The vehicle that will take data along the information highway is IP. For all of the reasons cited, this makes Web-based management the wave of the future at both the enterprise and the vendor levels.

There is a world of opportunity out there for the companies listed in this book, for innovative or disgruntled employees looking to get out on their own, or for other innovators to provide packages that will make Web-based network management faster, easier, cheaper, or more user-friendly. There is a market for software that will compile information. There is a market for software that will proactively go out and dig up data and return it at regular intervals. There is a huge market for security products. Many of these markets are specialty areas of existing product suites.

Customization and development of specific products is a given. There are many systems-specific products. A huge market area, for example, is point-of-sale (POS) systems. Every gas station, hotel, and retailer has a POS system. Every chain of grocery stores or fast-food restaurants has a POS system. Most of them are proprietary. Development of Web-based interfaces for any or all of them should prove a profitable venture. Such development will likely come from two sources. First, the savvy vendor soon will have a team working on Web-based access to such products (if such a team is not already in place). Second, impatient corporate users will develop Web-based management access systems and use them internally before their vendors bring such a system to market.

Beyond this, look at the different delivery media for information. Here, wireless is of prime interest. Wireless may be the next major wave in Web-based management. Computer Associates is looking at the wireless industry from two sides: First, there will be a demand to manage wireless and mobile devices; second, managing fixed devices by using wireless access tools will replace PC-based access in many cases. In both situations, there will be special needs for connectivity, and quality-of-transmission issues will have to be solved.

Predictive management will become more commonplace. In any network situation, it is far better to be able to predict an event before it occurs and deal with it before it becomes a minor disaster. Using today's technology, like the Motorola two-way pager, a device will be able to raise a network administrator and warn of a pending or current problem. These administrators will be able to handle simple problems from wherever they are standing—without even having to go off in search of a pay phone.

Look for Web-based enterprise management to go well beyond the realm of bridges and routers. Some firms already have systems on the market to manage non-IT devices. There is almost no limit to the number of these devices that can be tracked, monitored, reconfigured, or updated. Among the more commonplace examples are such things as elevators, refrigeration systems, the GPS (global positioning systems) which is used to track over-the-road trucks and monitor everything from the rig's location to fuel consumption and miles between transmission overhauls, and monitoring what is happening with the thousands of deep-well pumps generating supervisory control and data acquisition (SCADA) information for pipelines and other devices in the oil patch. It is easy to see how vital the continued performance of each of these systems is. There is also no reason why, with proper systems in place, a network manger should not be able to manage those devices from any IP-based terminal anywhere in the world.

Anything that can generate an SNMP trap—and that means almost any device that generates an electronic pulse—can generate a link to a management application.

Down the road, look for robots to become a part of the management system—on both ends of the inspection team. Because robots are basically specialized computers, they lend themselves to Web-based, or at least IP-based, management techniques. Beyond that, however, there is a strong likelihood that automated systems or robots will be part of the ongoing monitoring and restoration of many networks where the components are located in difficult-to-access areas, hazardous sites, or in locations (such as space stations or undersea research facilities) where humans simply can not commute handily. The array of instruments and computerized equipment in such environments is mind-boggling, and it all needs to be managed and replaced from time to time. A properly implemented Web-based system is ideal for handling such situations.

If you have come this far down the road of Web-based management with the author, you have a pretty good command of what is available, what to expect from a Web-based management system, and what potential pitfalls may be encountered when developing such a program.

Consider this your diploma from the basic course on Web-based network management. Now it's time to get back to the real world and apply what you have learned to make your enterprise management system more elegant and your life as a network manager easier to live.

Appendix: Vendor and Product Web Sites

The Web sites of the companies mentioned in this book were consulted and resources have been drawn from them.

VENDOR	PRODUCT	WEB ADDRESS
3Com, Inc.	Transcend Traffix Manager for Windows NT	www.3com.com/products /trans_net_man.html
ARESCOM, Inc.	Remote Manager	www.arescom.com
Asanté Technologies, Inc.	IntraSpection	www.asante.com
AT&T Solutions	Global Enterprise Management System (GEMS)	www.att.com/solutions
Bay Networks, Inc.	Optivity Network Management System	www.baynetworks.com
Boole & Babbage, Inc.	Explorer family	www.boole.com
Cabletron Systems	SPECTRUM Enterprise Manager	www.cabletron.com
Candle Corp.	ETEWatch	www.candle.com
Computer Associates International, Inc.	Unicenter TNG	www.cai.com
Concord Communications, Inc.	Network Health	www.concord.com
Edge Technologies, Inc.	edge N-Vision	www.edge-technologies .com

VENDOR	PRODUCT	WEB ADDRESS
Extreme Networks	ExtremeWare Enterprise Manager	www.extremenetworks.com
FastLane Technologies, Inc.	Virtual Administrator for Windows NT	www.fastlanetech.com
Fujitsu Network Communications, Inc.	Speedport FENS-AN	www.fnc.fujitsu.com
Hewlett-Packard Co.	HP TopTools HP BenchLink XL Software	www.hp.com
IBM Corp.	Nways Workgroup Manager	www.networking.ibm.com
INRANGE Technologies Corp.	INTERVIEW *DataWizard*	www.inrange.com
Jyra Research, Inc.	Service Management Architecture	www.jyra.com
Micromuse, Inc.	Netcool Suite	www.micromuse.com
NetOps Corp.	Do-It-Yourself (DIY) Network Analysis	www.netops.com
Net Scout Systems, Inc.	NetScout Manager Plus NetScout AppScout NetScout WebCast	www.netscout.com
Network Associates, Inc.	Sniffer Service Desk	www.nai.com
Novadigm, Inc.	Radia Software Manager	www.novadigm.com
Novazen, Inc.	Interactive Customer Care	www.novazen.com
Phasecom, Inc.	CyberManage for SpeedDemon	www.speed-demon.com
Pinnacle Software Corp.	Axis Web	www.pinnsoft.com
Sterling Software, Inc.	SOLVE:Netmaster for TCP/IP	www.solve.sterling.com
Telco Research Corp.	TRU Enterprise Network Accountant	www.telcoresearch.com
Tivoli Systems, Inc.	Distributed Monitoring	www.tivoli.com
Wipro Corp.	CyberManage	www.wipro.com
Xedia Corp.	Access Point	www.xedia.com

Bibliography

Books

Akermann, Ernest. *Learning to Use the World Wide Web.* Wilsonville, Ore.: Franklin, Beedle & Associates, 1996.

Bates, Bud. *Voice and Data Communications Handbook.* New York: McGraw-Hill, 1996.

Bradley, Layne C. *Handbook of Data Center Management.* Boston: Auerbach Publishers, 1990.

Carpentier, Michel. *Telecommunications in Transition.* New York: John Wiley & Sons, 1992.

Clark, Martin P. *Networks and Telecommunications.* New York: John Wiley & Sons, 1991.

Clayton, Jade. *Telecom Dictionary.* New York: McGraw-Hill, 1998.

Dern, Daniel P. *The Internet Guide for New Users.* New York: McGraw-Hill, 1994.

Downey, R., S. Boland, and P. Walsh. *Communications Technology Guide for Business.* Norwood, Mass.: Artech House, 1998.

Figallo, Cliff. *Hosting Web Communities.* New York: John Wiley & Sons, 1998.

Ferguson, P., and G. Huston. *Quality of Service.* New York: John Wiley & Sons, 1998.

Green, James Harry. *The Business One Irwin Handbook of Telecommunications.* Homewood, Ill.: Business One Irwin, 1992.

Grinberg, Arkady. *Computer/Telecom Integration.* New York: McGraw-Hill, 1995.

Hansen, Brad. *The Dictionary of Multimedia.* Wilsonville, Ore.: Franklin, Beedle & Associates, 1997.

Haywood, Martha. *Managing Virtual Teams.* Norwood: Artech House, 1998.

Held, Gilbert. *Network Management.* New York: John Wiley & Sons, 1992.

Huston, Geoff. *ISP Survival Guide.* New York: John Wiley & Sons, 1999.

Huurdeman, Anton. *Guide to Telecommunications Transmission Systems.* Norwood: Artech House, 1997.

Jewett, Jim. *Entrepreneurial Telecommunications.* Nashville, Tenn.: ES Press, 1989.

Kirvan, Paul. *Communications Management.* Turnersville, N.J.: Nelson Publishing, 1995.

Margulies, Ed. *Understanding the Voice-Enabled Internet.* New York: FlatIron Publishing, 1996.

Nemzow, Martin. *The Ethernet Management Guide.* New York: McGraw-Hill, 1995.

Newton, Harry. *Newton's Telecom Dictionary.* New York: FlatIron Publishing, 1996.

Nilles, Jack. *Making Telecommuting Happen.* New York: JALA International, 1994.

Opplinger, Rolf. *Internet and Intranet Security.* Norwood: Artech House, 1998.

Umar, Amjad. *Distributed Computing.* Englewood Cliffs, N.J.: P T R Prentice Hall, 1993.

Sexton, M., and A. Reid. *Broadband Networking: ATM, SDH, and SONET.* Norwood: Artech House, 1997.

Spohn, Darren. *Data Network Design.* New York: McGraw-Hill, 1997.

Taylor, D. Edgar. *The McGraw-Hill Internetworking Handbook.* New York: McGraw-Hill, 1995.

Ward, Ellen. *World-Class Telecommunications Service Development.* Norwood: Artech House, 1998.

Weber, Louis. *Home Computers.* Skokie, Ill.: Publications International, 1978.

Articles

Baltazar, Henry. "Virtual Administration Meets Today's NT Needs: Tool Lets Managers Delegate Chores." *PC Week,* February 16, 1998.

Biddlecombe, Elizabeth. "Browse Control." *Communications International,* June 1998.

"Demand For Network Management Software to Skyrocket." *Communications Today,* February 27, 1998.

Dukart, James R. "Extranets Are More Than the Internet's New Secret Societies. . . ." *Telephony,* March 16, 1998.

Flanagan, Patrick. "This Year's 10 Hottest Technologies in Telecom." *Telecommunications,* May 1998.

Harler, Curt. "The Good, The Bad, and the Fattening." *Americas Network,* June 1998.

Harler, Curt. "Web-Based Network Management." *Business Communications Review,* April 1998.

Harler, Curt. "Web-Based Reservations Come of Age." *Hospitality Technology,* July/August 1998.

Harler, C., and A. Stewart. "Interactive Bandwagon." *Communications International,* September 1997.

Herman, James. "Insights & Incites." *InternetWeek,* February 23, 1998.

Kennedy, Siobhan. "Enterprise Management Beckons." *Computer Weekly*, June 18, 1998.

Larson, Amy K. "Users Still Seek Turnkey Management Solutions." *InternetWeek*, January 5, 1998.

McCarthy, Shawn P. "Internet Management Packages Make Sense of Server Traffic Jam." *Government Computer News*, March 16, 1998.

Mullaney, Patrick. *The Simple Times: Quarterly Newsletter of SNMP* 4(3), July 1996.

Musigh, Paula. "Micromuse Tool Monitors Multiple Firewalls." *PC Week*, September 14, 1998.

Wellers, C. and K. Auerbach. *The Simple Times: Quarterly Newsletter of SNMP* 5(1), December 1997.

Wilson, Tim. "Telepath." *InternetWeek*, March 2, 1998.

Wong, William. "Around the Globe with Network Management." *Network VAR*, March 1, 1998.

White Papers

Bay Networks, Incorporated. "Optivity Management." Santa Clara, Calif., 1998.

Candle Corporation. "End-to-End Application Response Time Monitoring." Santa Monica, Calif., 1998.

Fast Lane Technologies, Incorporated. "Using Virtual Administration Tool to Delegate Administration in Enterprise Windows NT Server Networks." Halifax, Nova Scotia, Canada, August 1998.

Huntington-Lee, J. "Controlling A Decentralized Environment." San Francisco, Calif., May 1997.

Huntington-Lee, J., and A. Thomas. "Delivering Service to a Major ISP." San Francisco, Calif., 1997.

Hurwitz Group. "Unicenter TND: It's about Time." Framingham, Mass., April 1998.

Ibrahim, Erfan. "A Comparative Analysis of Embedded Probe Versus External Agents for Applications Response Time Monitoring." San Jose, Calif.: Jyra Research, October 1998.

McConnell, John. "Remote Network Monitoring" Boulder, CO

Tribble, Bud. "Java Computing in the Enterprise." Sun Microsystems, 1996.

Acronyms Used in This Book

API	Application Program Interfaces
CBQ	Customer-Based Quality
CEO	Chief Executive Officer
CERT	Computer Emergency Response Team
CFO	Chief Financial Officer
CGI	Common Gateway Interface
CIM	Common Information Model
CIO	Chief Information Officer
CORBA	Common Object Request Broker Architecture
DHCP	Dynamic Host Configuration Protocol
DIY	Do It Yourself
DMI	Desktop Management Interface
DMTF	Desktop Management Task Force
DNS	Domain Name System
DSL	Digital Subscriber Lines
DSM	Digital Signal Monitors
GPS	Global Positioning Systems
GUI	Graphical User Interface
HTML	Hypertext Markup Language
HTTP	Hypertext Transfer Protocol

HTTPD	Hypertext Transfer Protocol Daemon
IETF	Internet Engineering Task Force
IP	Internet Protocol
IP-PBX	Internet Protocol-Private Branch Exchange
IS	Information Systems
ISDN	Integrated Services Digital Network
ISO	International Organization for Standardization
ISP	Internet Service Provider
IT	Information Technology
JDBC	Java Database Connectivity Protocol
LAN	Local Area Network
LDAP	Lightweight Directory Access Protocol
MIB	Management Information Base
MIS	Management Information Systems
NMS	Network Management Systems
OLTP	Online Transaction Processing
OSI	Open Systems Interconnection
PBX	Private Branch Exchange
POS	Point of Sale
QoS	Quality of Service
RFC	Request for Comment
RFP	Request for Proposal
RFQ	Request for Quotation
RMON	Remote Network Monitoring
RPC	Remote Procedure Call
SCADA	Supervisory Control and Data Acquisition
SDK	Software Development Kit
SGML	Standard Generalized Markup Language
SLA	Service Level Agreement
SNMP	Simple Network Management Protocol
SQL	Structured Query Language

SYSOP	System Operator
TCP/IP	Transmission Control Protocol/Internet Protocol
UDP	User Datagram Protocol
URL	Uniform Resource Locator
VLAN	Virtual Local Area Network
VRML	Virtual Reality Markup Language
WAN	Wide Area Network
WBEM	Web-Based Enterprise Management
WWW	World Wide Web
xDSL	Any Digital Subscriber Lines
XML	Extensible Markup Language

Index